Advance

The demands of our day ~~~~~~~~~~~~ our attention. Naomi Vacaro ~~~~~~~~~~~~~~~~~~~~ our desperate need for quiet time with Jesus. Written with warmth, kindness, and understanding, this book will help you develop patterns of Bible reading and prayer that will grow your love for God and for others.

MELISSA KRUGER
Author and director of women's initiatives for The Gospel Coalition

If you've ever struggled with feeling like a quiet-time failure, this book will offer you a helping hand and tangible tools to stir your love for Jesus. In *Quiet*, Naomi Vacaro spurs us on toward a life that is fueled by God's grace and a love for his Word. By sharing her own story of leaving behind the weight of drudgery to grasp the delight of following God, Naomi beautifully illustrates how a quiet time is a gift of grace that roots our souls deeply in unchanging truth.

GRETCHEN SAFFLES
Bestselling author of *The Well-Watered Woman: Rooted in Truth, Growing in Grace, Flourishing in Faith* and founder of Well-Watered Women

This book offers a much-needed reminder to slow down and be quiet before the Lord. In our fast-paced, entertainment-driven, microwave society, we need to be reminded of what's most important: daily time with our Creator and Savior. *Quiet* is a book for every woman who desires to know Jesus in a deeper and more intimate way. If you want true rest and peace for your soul, this book is for you!

This is such a wonderful resource for women who desire to grow in consistently spending time with the Lord. Naomi beautifully weaves her life story through these pages to illustrate the journey of growing in our love for and daily pursuit of Christ. It's a book you'll want both for yourself and to pass along to others.

We all know we should be reading our Bibles more, but we often become distracted by the busyness of life and discouraged by our failures. We expect our quiet times to be perfect, complete with a comfy chair, a flickering candle, hot coffee, and ... quiet. But creating these magical moments can feel like an impossible task, so we give up—or never even start. Naomi knows the struggle is real, but so is our God. In her book, *Quiet*, she equips you to dive deeper into God's Word, create sticky quiet-time habits, and develop a more devoted walk with God. This book is packed with practical tips, engaging stories, and insightful connections. Whether you're an avid Bible reader or just getting started, this book will help you grow and encourage your heart.

Anyone who has battled guilt, drudgery, or unexplainable distance in their quiet times will be refreshed by Naomi's humble approach to this consistent problem. So many of us settle into a rut with no hope of climbing out, assuming steady and joy-filled quiet times aren't available to us. *Quiet* helps readers explore the root of the distance through thoughtful reflection and prayer, leaving us surrendered, refocused, and ready to pursue the Lord through his Word with a new perspective.

KATIE GUILIANO
Founder and artist at Hosanna Revival

Quiet is a beautiful and encouraging book that offers a fresh vision and practical advice for building daily intimacy with Christ. In our fast-paced world, having a regular quiet time can often feel more like a burden than a delight. This book brings us back to the heart of what spending time with Jesus is really all about.

LESLIE LUDY
Bestselling author of *Authentic Beauty* and *The Set-Apart Woman*

We need God, yet most of us are fumbling through how to find him these days as the world tilts. This book is that hand from a friend—outstretched, ready to hold ours and walk us through how to find him in his Word . . . again or for the first time. What a gift!

SARA HAGERTY
Bestselling author of *Unseen: The Gift of Being Hidden in a World that Loves to Be Noticed* and *Adore: A Simple Practice for Experiencing God in the Middle Minutes of Your Day*

Creating Grace-Based Rhythms
for Spending Time with Jesus

quiet

Naomi Vacaro

Creator of the Wholehearted Community

TYNDALE
MOMENTUM®

A Tyndale nonfiction imprint

Visit Tyndale online at tyndale.com.

Visit Tyndale Momentum online at tyndalemomentum.com.

Visit the author at wholeheartedquiettime.com.

Tyndale, Tyndale's quill logo, *Tyndale Momentum*, and the Tyndale Momentum logo are registered trademarks of Tyndale House Ministries. Tyndale Momentum is a nonfiction imprint of Tyndale House Publishers, Carol Stream, Illinois.

Quiet: Creating Grace-Based Rhythms for Spending Time with Jesus

Designed by Eva M. Winters

Edited by Stephanie Rische

For information about special discounts for bulk purchases, please contact Tyndale House Publishers at csresponse@tyndale.com, or call 1-855-277-9400.

Library of Congress Cataloging-in-Publication Data

A catalog record for this book is available from the Library of Congress.

ISBN 978-1-4964-5332-7

Printed in the United States of America

28	27	26	25	24	23	22
7	6	5	4	3	2	1

To Mom and Dad. Your daily faithfulness
is what led me to Christ.
And to Matt. Your servant-leadership is
what made this book possible.

contents

Foreword by Phylicia Masonheimer *xi*

Introduction *1*

1 Where It All Begins:
Our Desperate Need for Jesus **11**

2 Guilt and Grace:
When We Fail to Have a Quiet Time **29**

3 Drudgery, Discipline, and Delight:
The Emotional Stages of a Quiet Time **41**

4 The Most Important Habit:
Making Jesus Part of Our Everyday Lives **65**

5 Reading the Bible:
Loving and Living God's Word **85**

6 Talking with Jesus:
Becoming a Prayer Warrior **105**

7 Getting Creative:
*Quiet-Time Ruts and How to Get Out
of Them* **127**

8 Letting the Lord Lead:
The Holy Spirit's Role in Our Quiet Time **147**

9 Changing Seasons:
*Adapting Our Quiet Times to Our
Circumstances* **165**

10 Quiet Time in Community:
    Our Need for Christ-Centered Fellowship **185**

11 The Ripple Effect:
    *Having a Quiet Time Impacts Everyone
    around Us* **201**

12 Wholehearted Love:
    So Much More than a Quiet Time **219**

Appendix: Recommended Resources **231**

Acknowledgments **235**

Notes **239**

About the Author **241**

foreword

MY HIGH SCHOOL QUIET TIME was the stuff of legend. It was a war room before *War Room* was a movie. It had a (very trendy) CD player and a pile of Avalon albums, an entire wall of prayer request cards, and a basketful of Bible study materials, pens, and paper. Freshly devoted to Christ at age fifteen, I spent an hour each morning in my walk-in closet. My faith grew, my heart was opened to the Lord's work, and foundations were laid. I learned how to study the Bible for myself and how to talk to God as a father and a friend. That closet was my refuge, a safe place to grow.

Then I went to college. I got married. My career took off. I had a baby . . . then two . . . then three.

Life has changed drastically since those days in my walk-in closet. My "quiet time" now takes place on my living room couch. Sometimes I'm joined by one or more children, other times by my husband. Many times it's not quiet at all! There are days I don't get to it in the morning, so I'm bent over a Bible in the afternoon, pens and notebook spread across the dining room table. There have been times when all I did was whisper a prayer while collecting the eggs and sweeping the porch, my Bible opened to Psalms in a cookbook holder.

My time with God has morphed a hundred times over the years. Instead of losing quality as it loses perfection, our relationship has grown all the richer because of the changes. Since the first time I read through the whole Bible, I've seen how the truths of God's Word meet us in every season, transition, and change. Daily habits of study, prayer, and worship do not need perfect circumstances to survive; they only need a willing heart. As I approach the Lord day after day, season upon season, embracing—rather than resisting—the changes, I find a faith immovable. Firmly planted, like a tree.

My dad taught me a lot about the Bible as a child but only made me memorize one passage: Psalm 1. It's the passage I say under my breath when I'm anxious, angry, or afraid. The righteous are "like a tree planted by streams of water, which yields its fruit in season" (verse 3). This image of a mighty oak reaching its roots into living water grants a glimpse of what the minutes in God's presence do to our hearts. His work is unseen. It's almost always slow. But isn't that how growth goes? It's an imperceptible expansion until—when the season is right—we bear fruit.

Our need for God is constant. Our circumstances, not so much. I've learned to embrace a quiet time that is less about the quiet of my house and more about the quiet of my spirit. Will I stop running long enough to listen? Will I still my soul to hear his voice? Will I be like a tree (or like a branch on the Vine) and let him bear fruit in me?

These are the questions Naomi asks in this book. On the following pages you will be gently led toward a time with God that is sustainable but also beautiful, fulfilling, and built to last. Many books will tell you to read the Bible more; Naomi will show you how. She will walk with you every step of the way. I hope you're blessed, like I was, to learn the sweetness of quietness in Christ—even when your life is anything but quiet.

Phylicia Masonheimer
Founder and CEO, Every Woman a Theologian

introduction

THE MORNING LIGHT IS JUST ARRIVING as I sit at my dining room table and write these words. It's the rainy season here in Florida, and yesterday brought torrential downpours for hours on end. Today the sky has cleared, and the sun is starting to peek over the horizon. The birds are beginning to sing as the humidity slowly evaporates from the windows, revealing a scene of sparkling leaves and vibrant blossoms outside.

All around our little home stand massive oak trees. Their branches extend toward the heavens while their roots spread beneath the neighborhood, holding together the soil and pushing up against the brick and pavement. These trees have been here for decades, some for more than a hundred years. Every year they seem to grow a little taller, a little wider, and a little greener. When I look at these trees, I think of Jeremiah 17:7-8:

> Blessed are those who trust in the LORD and have made the LORD their hope and confidence. They are like trees planted along a riverbank, with roots that reach deep into the water. Such trees are not bothered by the heat or worried by long months of drought. Their leaves stay green and they never stop producing fruit. (NLT)

I have always wanted to be a deeply rooted Christian. Ever since I read this passage as a child, I've prayed that I would be like the tree in Jeremiah 17, quietly unwavering in my faithfulness to the Lord. I have seen examples of this steadfastness firsthand in the hard-working believers I grew up with on the mission field in Mongolia, the women who attend my Thursday-night prayer group, the older members of my church who arrive to worship with tattered Bibles, and especially my own mother, father, sisters, and brothers. These believers seem like trees to me, planted next to the stream of life, flourishing more every year as their hope in the Lord grows and deepens.

I've often wondered though: What is it that sets these saints apart?

Deep Roots

In late 2017, Hurricane Irma tore through our city in Florida. I'll never forget that night. My husband, Matt, and I, along with my siblings and their spouses, gathered at my parents' home and slept on the living room floor as the wind howled outside and nearby branches groaned and then cracked like shots in the dark. When we emerged the following morning, the world looked like a war zone. The streets were so littered with debris that you could hardly see the pavement. Lines were down, electricity was out, and an eerie quiet had settled over the neighborhood.

But what I remember most were the felled trees. Trees that had stood four stories high the day before now lay vertical, their entire root systems torn up and exposed. These downed monsters were now blocking roads, upturning sidewalks, and crushing houses. However, not every tree had fallen. Many of the trees in our neighborhood remained standing, including the giant oak just outside our front door.

Shortly after the hurricane, my older sister, Emily, wrote a blog post explaining the difference between the felled trees and the trees that remained standing:

> There are two types of oak trees [in Central Florida]: live oaks and water oaks. They both grow to about eighty feet tall, host a variety of birds and animals in their sturdy branches, and provide more than enough shade with their leafy limbs. On the surface

it's hard to tell the difference, until a hurricane comes along. Water oaks like the sun and take the rain for granted. Why grow deep roots when water is plentiful? They shoot up quickly and stand alone, tall and magnificent. Live oaks grow slower and focus their energy on sending their roots deep into the ground.[1]

The depth of their roots had made the difference between life and death for these trees, and after Hurricane Irma, it became clear which had shallow roots and which had roots that were secure enough to weather the storm.

These water oaks and live oaks, with their shallow or deep roots, reflect the life of our Christian faith. If we're water-oak Christians, then we are planted in the shallow soil of cultural Christianity. We may look like we're flourishing on the outside, but time and testing eventually reveal that the soil beneath us is nothing but the shifting sands of worldly trends. A water-oak Christian seeks nourishment in things that will never satisfy, like success, popularity, outward appearance, or momentary pleasure. We might go through the motions of faith, but ultimately we lack a genuine and transformative relationship with the person of Jesus. When the winds of persecution or the seductive breeze of temptation blow, we become uprooted, just like the water oaks did.

In contrast, when we are living as live-oak Christians, we sink our roots into the bedrock of Jesus Christ. We grow slowly and steadily, and we build our lives on the foundation of God's Word. We are quietly committed to following Jesus Christ no matter what. When persecution arrives, we only grow stronger in the faith. When temptation knocks, we refuse to be uprooted by lies and misguided loves.

These deeply rooted followers of Jesus can be found all across the globe. They have different personalities, backgrounds, cultures, ages, life stages, and experiences. But there's one thing they all have in common: they read the Bible and pray.

I would venture to say that there is no mature believer in Christ who does not read their Bible and pray on a regular basis. While a relationship with Jesus is definitely *more* than a daily quiet time, it is certainly not *less*.

The primary way we become rooted, live-oak Christians is by spending time with Jesus. We can't grow in our understanding of and love for God without reading the Bible, and we can't develop a genuine closeness with Christ if we don't communicate with him in prayer. Without the regular habit of a quiet time, we will become spiritually malnourished and eventually starve. Just as trees need soil and water to grow, we need spiritual nutrients for our faith to mature and deepen.

> *While a relationship with Jesus is definitely more than a daily quiet time, it is certainly not less.*

The truth is, we have all been shallow-rooted, water-oak Christians at some point in our lives. Deep roots take time to grow, and the consistent habits of Bible reading and prayer simply don't happen overnight. But no matter how dried up we may feel in our current season, Jesus can deepen our roots and bring us—and our love for spending time with him—back to life.

I know it's true, because I've lived it.

Grace-Based Quiet Time

Maybe you've always struggled to read your Bible and pray. Maybe having a daily quiet time is a brand-new idea to you. Maybe this is something you used to do consistently but the circumstances of your life have changed, and now it feels like your relationship with Jesus is falling apart. Maybe every time you hear the words *quiet time*, you bristle with unspoken shame.

Or maybe it's the *quiet* part of "quiet time" that makes your hands get sweaty. In this season of your life, you'd be happy to squeeze in a shower without someone needing you, and the idea of doing anything that resembles stillness seems far-fetched. If *quiet* is a requirement, then you feel like you've failed.

Trust me, I get it.

Having a daily quiet time is something I've struggled with all my life. Growing up in a Christian home taught me *why* it was important to read the Bible and pray, but for some reason, I just couldn't form the regular habit. I saw my lack of consistency as spiritual disobedience, and as a result, guilt gnawed at my soul for years.

Things got better in college when my quiet time became

more consistent. Reading the Bible and praying every day became a routine I genuinely enjoyed and even looked forward to. The habit survived my transition into married life a couple of years after graduation. With a flexible schedule and lots of free time on my hands, it was easier than ever to read the Bible and pray.

Then I became a mother.

Once I had a baby in my arms, my habit of Bible reading and prayer completely fell apart. Instead of reading three chapters a day, I barely opened my Bible once a week. Instead of hour-long conversations with Jesus, my prayer time consisted of impromptu breakdowns as I bounced a crying baby on my hip. At first I found this alarming. Where had all my hardearned consistency disappeared to? I was tempted to despair, but the Lord was teaching me yet another profound lesson about grace.

Even before I became a mother, I was starting to realize I'd been treating my relationship with God like a performance. Deep down, I'd been viewing Bible reading and prayer as a way to earn God's approval instead of a way to nourish my own soul. Instead of leading me closer to Jesus, my guilt was making it harder for me to come to the Lord. By the time I became a mother and my quiet time had to be completely restructured, I was ready to silence the voice of shame in my soul and embrace the quiet waters of grace.

> *God doesn't keep a tally of all the days, weeks, and months you haven't spent time with him.*

I was ready to have a grace-based quiet time.

Having a quiet time that's built on grace means your Bible will still be available to read tomorrow morning even if you don't get to read it today. It means you don't have to play catch-up in order to get back on track with your quiet time. It means God doesn't keep a tally of all the days, weeks, and months you've failed to spend time with him. It means there will be seasons when coming to Jesus is more difficult—and he delights in you anyway. It means that yesterday's failure does not diminish today's opportunity to know and enjoy Jesus.

Yesterday's failure does not diminish today's opportunity to know and enjoy Jesus.

If this idea of a grace-based quiet time sounds good to you, then you're reading the right book. Wherever you happen to be right now in your relationship with Jesus, I want you to know that this isn't about dredging up your shortcomings or convincing you of what a failure you are for not reading your Bible every day. This book is about restoring your eagerness to walk with Jesus. It's about equipping you to create spiritual rhythms that have the power to transform your life.

These pages are filled with stories from my own journey, along with lessons I've learned about spending time with Jesus over the years. Sprinkled throughout the chapters, you'll find sidebars with quiet-time stories from women in various walks of life. I have also included practical ideas to help you create and maintain a quiet time yourself, no matter what season you happen to be in. For those who want to dig deeper, each chapter also includes questions to reflect on, ways to grow, and prayers to pray.

I didn't write this book because I have all the answers or because I perfectly practice the habit of a quiet time. I wrote this book because I've experienced the crushing load of quiet-time guilt myself, and yet I've seen that it is possible, by the grace and power of God, to break free from frustration and failure and start enjoying a consistent and fruitful relationship with Jesus. The quiet our souls long for is well within reach.

Naomi Vacaro
SPRING 2022

1

where it all begins

Our Desperate Need for Jesus

"HAVE YOU HAD YOUR QUIET TIME YET TODAY?"

I looked up to see my mom's face peering around the corner. I was a restless, homeschooled seven-year-old at the time. It was getting late in the afternoon, and I was trying to finish my assignments before the sun went down. Since my mom had made daily devotions a part of my curriculum, this question was one I had come to dread.

Had I had my quiet time yet? No. Would I? Yes, because only then would I be allowed to play outside, an activity I enjoyed far more than reading the Bible. I informed my mom that I was, in fact, just about to have my quiet time, and she smiled knowingly before leaving me to complete the task.

Bible reading was the part of daily devotions I dreaded most, so I tackled it first to get it over with. I skimmed the pages of my children's Bible just enough to absorb the pictures and be ready to answer any questions my mom might ask later. Then I moved on to prayer. I'd been taught to close my eyes and bow my head, so that's what I did, mumbling words that only God now remembers. Then, with a final "Amen!" I opened my eyes and jumped to my feet. Freedom was waiting!

The Mongolian sun was just beginning to set over the dusty hills as I grabbed a dog leash and burst through the front door. The leash was unnecessary since I wasn't going anywhere and our yard was completely surrounded by a tall fence topped with barbed wire. Fences like this were typical for the Mongolian homes all around us, but the concept of walking a dog was definitely not. Dogs here were meant for guarding property, not parading around on a leash. That didn't matter to me, though. I had seen American movies that depicted people walking their dogs, and using a leash made me feel like a grown-up. So, I coaxed our scraggly mutt out of her doghouse and into a collar. As Poko and I made our way around the yard, the sun began to cast long shadows and paint the Mongolian dirt a deep shade of orange.

This dry patch of earth had been my home for two years. Before we moved here, my family and I had lived in a Soviet-style apartment building near the center of Ulaanbaatar, Mongolia's capital city. Most of the buildings in Ulaanbaatar were Russian made, expressionless and efficient, a reminder of who had built the city and who had, until recently, controlled the lives of its occupants. By the 1990s, most Russians had departed Mongolia. However, they left behind a Communist mentality that lingered for years to come. The country had been closed to outsiders for generations, and it wasn't until 1990 that Mongolia's doors swung open to allow foreigners to enter freely.

My parents were some of the first in line.

Tom and Lynn Suchy felt called to become missionaries to this cold, developing nation, so they packed their belongings and their children and boarded a flight to Mongolia in 1993. There were only four of us back then: my mom and dad, my almost-three-year-old sister, and nine-month-old me. Within six years, two more kids were added to our family. In 1998 we left the Soviet-style

Judy's Quiet-Time Story

My quiet times have looked different in different seasons. When I had small children, I learned that God didn't care if my quiet time didn't look the way I thought it should. I placed Bibles in several key places around the house—I even had one in my car! More often than not, my quiet time consisted of standing in my kitchen with a Bible open, surrounded by a mess and a couple of kids. I stopped thinking there was only one way to have a quiet time. Sometimes it wasn't very quiet! Other days my time with the Lord was long and truly quieting for my soul. Sometimes I study deeply and read and pray, and other days my quiet time is brief. I know God doesn't judge me for how I experience time with him. I can't imagine how much more difficult the past three decades would have been if not for the ability to cry out to God and hold on to him in the midst of my challenges and sorrows.

apartment building in the city and moved into a new home—a house made of straw bales covered with stucco.

The Straw Bale House, as we called it, was tucked away among the hills, about four miles northeast of the city. My dad had built our home himself with the help of several Mongolian friends, and now it was our own little sanctuary. We planted a modest garden by the front entrance, dug an outhouse near the far corner of the property, and built a woodshed to store the never-ending supply of logs needed to keep our house warm during the winter, when temperatures reached negative thirty degrees and colder.

As foreigners, we were not allowed to own property, so a Mongolian family let us build the Straw Bale House on their land. The area was nearly a half-acre and a dream for an imaginative, rambunctious child like me.

It didn't take long for my siblings and me to discover that the Straw Bale House stood on land that was filled with treasures. The property had once been used as a slaughter ground for animals, and we delightedly dug up bones and other unidentifiable objects to store in secret places. One summer we pretended we were archaeologists and set our treasures on display in a "museum" for our parents and their occasional visitors to look at for the thoughtfully calculated price of one hundred Tugrik. (At the time, one hundred Tugrik would have been the equivalent of eleven cents in US currency.)

The Straw Bale House quickly became my beloved childhood home.

A Sunset Stroll

That evening when I was marching our reluctant dog around on her leash, I suffered no guilt about having rushed through my quiet time moments earlier. I didn't know why I needed to read the Bible and pray in the first place—I thought of it as merely an expectation my parents had of me.

My mom and dad took their role as parents even more seriously than their calling as missionaries. If there was one thing they persistently taught us kids, it was that spending time with Jesus was a necessary part of everyday life. Since I was a natural-born people pleaser, I tried my best to comply with their desires, albeit with an abundance of grumbling.

I wore the label "missionary kid" proudly. I enjoyed the unique story of my life, along with the wide-eyed looks people gave me in America when I told them where I lived. Most significantly, though, I was convinced that being a missionary kid gave me spiritual value. I assumed that my parents' self-sacrifice and passion for the gospel somehow secured my own spot in the lineup of saints who would one day go marching into glory. Our role as missionaries became my identity. Having a daily quiet time came with the territory, and it was a small price to pay for me to be the missionary kid I was supposed to be.

So there I was, seven years old and proud as could be, strolling around in my Mongolian yard. I was entirely unaware that I was lacking a genuine relationship with Jesus

Christ. But God wasn't about to let me stay comfortable in my own delusions.

As I dragged a confused but happy Poko around the corner of our storage container, the sunset suddenly captured my gaze and forced my feet to an abrupt halt. My breath left me as rays of light caught the dust around the yard, transforming the particles into tiny flecks of floating gold. The summer breeze brushed against my arms and face, filling my nose with the scent of distant wildflowers. The heavens were lit up in rich reds and yellows, and the clouds painted a celestial city in the sky. I was overwhelmed by a sense of awe.

As I stood transfixed, I knew instinctively that the beauty before me was not a *what* but a *who*. For the first time in my young life, I felt the presence of Jesus as an undeniable reality. Though my eyes didn't see him, Christ shone before my soul as clearly as the sunset. Instantly, the awareness of my great need rushed through me and I perceived my sinfulness clearly for the first time. Though I felt completely exposed before the Holy One, I also knew instinctively that I was *fully loved*. A desperate longing overtook me, and at the same time, contentment spread through me like a sigh of relief. I sensed that Jesus was presenting himself as the answer to my soul's thirst, the definition of my identity, and the purpose for my future. Jesus was beckoning.

There in that dusty yard, beneath a Mongolian sunset, with tiny hands clutching a dog leash, I gave my life to Jesus. It felt like he had caught me up in his arms and claimed me as his own. Although my seven-year-old mind couldn't grasp the magnitude of that moment, I knew Jesus had completely swept me away and nothing would ever be the same.

Budding Faith

A year after that soul-transforming moment, I was living in Wisconsin. Our family had recently packed our belongings, boarded up the Straw Bale House, and flown to America for a year. We had churches to visit and support to raise if we were going to continue our work as missionaries.

I was reeling from the transition. We had been living in America for several months, and I longed for the familiar sights and smells of home. I deeply missed the friends I'd left behind in Mongolia. A year may not be long for an adult, but it feels like an eternity for an eight-year-old.

Rachel's Quiet-Time Story

I struggle with thinking that I have to spend a certain amount of time praying or reading the Bible every day, or that a quiet time is just another item on a long list of things I need to do to have a good day. I buy into the lie that if I can't do it well enough, it's not worth doing at all. The burden I carry when I fall short is not what God wants for me. But through it all, I have experienced so much grace. God is patient to take all my mess and turn it into something beautiful. He assures me that his righteousness alone is what I must rest in—it's not my acts, but the Holy Spirit cleansing me. His grace is irresistible!

Wisconsin looked like the rest of America to me. Every town had the same McDonald's on the corner, the same residential neighborhoods with manicured lawns, and the same endless stretches of highway in between. The air smelled clean and fresh—so unlike the scents of dust, smoke, and mutton back home.

I clung to my siblings wherever we went. I especially dreaded Sunday mornings, when the four of us were sent off to various classrooms for children's services. In the halls of megachurches and the pews of chapels, I was stared at not for the color of my skin, as I had been in Mongolia, but for being the missionary kid whose father would be giving a talk after the main service ended.

While part of me enjoyed the attention, I mostly felt exotic, strange, and unable to relate to the other children. It didn't take long for me to decide that I much preferred standing out as a white person in an Asian country than as a stranger in an American youth group.

At the time, the routine of Bible reading and prayer was still mostly a chore for me. The one activity I consistently enjoyed was journaling. I loved writing in my diary—a book that locked on the outside and shimmered with glitter that never quite left my fingers. Within those pages, I recorded my deepest and most private thoughts: my current crushes, my desperate longings, and my child-like prayers.

I believed that all was well in my relationship with Jesus. I thought that God cared for and loved me if I lived in obedience to him. I knew I wasn't without sin, but I didn't think I had any major flaws that would keep me from approaching the Father. I thought his approval was based on my moral performance, particularly my faithfulness in having a quiet time—a spiritual duty I took very seriously. In my budding faith, I unconsciously created a system of give-and-take, and the system seemed to work.

Until it didn't.

Secret Shame

I'll never forget that quiet, seemingly harmless night in our Wisconsin home. I was sitting at the desk in our dining room, innocently exploring the internet on our family computer. Suddenly, an unsolicited image lit up the screen. No one else was around to explain what glowed in front of me or to help me make a quick and decisive exit. Although I was too young to understand what I saw, the image piqued a deep curiosity within me, as well as a faint nudge in my conscience.

I spent many evenings that year trying to sneak back onto the computer when no one was looking. As my addictive curiosity grew, so did the deep, aching guilt within my spirit. How could I pray or read my Bible when I'd just viewed something so inappropriate? How would Jesus accept me now? These questions revealed my true confusion over God's grace and my position in Christ.

My soul was miserably stuck during that year in America,

and I brought my soul sickness with me across the ocean when we returned to Mongolia. As the days turned into months, and as the months turned into years, the secret sin continued, and my spirituality became rooted in shame. When I experienced seasons of greater self-control, I would open my Bible and pray with peace of mind. I was winning the battle against sin! Surely this would make me thoroughly "quiet-time approved." Eventually, though, the hidden door would creak open, and the subsequent shame would cause me to avoid prayer altogether. I wouldn't even pick up my Bible until enough time had passed since my previous infraction. The best way I could think of to punish myself was by putting distance between God's perfection and my filth. This pattern of pride and shame repeated itself for years.

I can see now that my understanding of Jesus was fundamentally skewed. I saw him as the hand I'd shaken to get through the door of salvation, but then I assumed that the rest of the Christian walk was up to me. I assumed it was my efforts that secured my position with God, whether that meant having a daily quiet time, going to church, or praying before dinner. This way of thinking also meant that every failure, large and small, was equally my responsibility. I began to wonder, *Am I really a Christian? What would God do to punish me for this sin?*

My enjoyment of Christ became entirely based on my own inconsistent performance. I was dying inside, knowing that all my efforts would never ever be enough.

The Lie of Self-Sufficiency

Perhaps you've been there yourself. The specifics of your situation may be different—maybe for you the struggle is with food or envy or control or the approval of others. But at some point you realize that as hard as you try, you can't muscle your way into God's favor. No matter how much discipline you can muster, self-sufficiency is nothing more than delusion.

We see this delusion play out in the opening pages of the Bible, when Adam and Eve, our first parents, listen to the lies of the serpent and rebel against their Creator. Though they were created perfectly good and were placed in a world full of wonderful possibilities, they decided to distrust and disobey God. The result was catastrophe . . . for *all* of us.

As hard as we try, we can't muscle our way into God's favor. Only grace can bring us there.

Just as we inherit the physical traits of our parents, we are born with the same spiritual condition of the generations before us. Just as our first parents chose self-sufficiency, we, too, buy the lie that we can manage life just fine without God and can handle guilt and shame through our own means.

Though I had accepted Jesus as my Savior, I still acted as though I could earn his approval through my own efforts. I couldn't admit my sin, because that would mean I'd failed, and that would mean I wouldn't make the cut with God. Just like Adam and Eve, I believed more in my own competence than in God's goodness. Just like Adam and Eve, I was trying to cover my shame and failure behind flimsy leaves.

But God didn't give up on the people who rebelled against him thousands of years ago. And he doesn't give up on us, either.

His Skin for Mine

Although God was no doubt heartbroken over Adam and Eve's rebellion, he responded with calmness and grace. While they hid in shame, God sought them out to address their disobedience, spell out the rightful consequences of their rebellion, and mercifully make provision for their nakedness.

> The LORD God made for Adam and for his wife garments of skins and clothed them.
> GENESIS 3:21, ESV

I was just a child when I first witnessed the slaughter and skinning of a sheep. It's a common occurrence in Mongolia, where people have been surviving off their animals for thousands of years. First, the sheep is tied up and dragged, wide eyed and panicked, to a designated spot, usually a grassy area. It's then methodically relieved of its life. I'll spare you the details, but I will say it's impossible not to get your hands dirty in the process.

It's humbling to imagine God himself entering into this bloody, messy business in the middle of his perfect Garden. Adam and Eve had just committed high treason by trying to usurp God's place as ruler of his world. While God slayed the animal, Adam and Eve stood nearby in shame, with a new awareness of their nakedness—a nakedness they tried to cover with leaves. Though they should have been killed on the spot, he showed them mercy and spared their lives. He killed an animal instead, skinned it, and covered Adam and Eve.

Thousands of years later, another bloody scene unfolded. Instead of an animal, God's perfect Son was stripped naked, whipped, tortured, and put to death on behalf of sinners like you and me. When Jesus died on the cross, he did so as our substitute, bearing the punishment that rightfully belonged to Adam, Eve, and all their offspring. Through Jesus' death, the greatness of God's love was displayed, and our sin and shame were dealt with once and for all. When Jesus rose from the dead three days later, sin was atoned for, the lying serpent was crushed, and the door to everlasting life was opened. God's goodness, love, and power were proven once and for all.

When we acknowledge that we can never be good enough on our own, we are set free to come to Jesus as we are.

This is the Good News: we stand as naked and helpless as Adam and Eve, but in Jesus, we are offered a covering provided by God. When we acknowledge that we can never be good enough to be right with God on our own and choose instead to trust in the work of Christ, we are

The Cross gives sinners the chance to be saints and orphans the opportunity to become daughters.

set free from guilt and can begin to experience God's transforming grace. Instead of hiding from God, we can run right to him! God welcomes us to come to him like little children who constantly admit to their Father how much they need his help. Praise the Lord! The Cross gives sinners the chance to be saints, paupers the chance to be princes and princesses, and orphans the opportunity to become sons and daughters.

Broken Chains

As a teenager, I desperately needed to understand the gospel so I could apply it to my struggles. My faith was at a crossroads: either I could continue in secret sin and shame, or I could step out in faith and reveal my sin. The latter option was appalling to my people-pleasing mentality. But I was also miserable. I couldn't stand the thought of living in the darkness any longer.

It was six in the morning at the Straw Bale House when I stepped softly into the living room. Though it was still dark and the cold spring wind was blowing, I knew my mom would be up with a fire burning. Sure enough, she was sitting by the wood stove with her Bible and journal open, busily writing down what I knew were prayers for the many people she loved.

As I approached her, my heart thudded inside my chest and my feet threatened to turn back. Ignoring my nerves, I took a deep breath.

"Mom, can we talk?"

She immediately agreed. She asked no questions as she followed me into my bedroom. She sat beside me on my bed as I began to unlock the hidden door to my heart.

Tears ran down my face as I choked through my confession. As my words tumbled out, my soul began to stir with the sweet relief of an unburdened conscience.

My mom took my hands into hers, and the tears on her face matched my own. Her eyes glowed with an unconditional love that sent my fear fleeing. When she opened her mouth, words of grace, love, and assurance poured out. She told me that my act of confession was proof that the Holy Spirit was doing a great work in my heart that day. She also said that nothing would affect her love for me, regardless of what wrongs lay in my past or future.

In that moment I stepped into freedom, and the power of my secret sin was officially broken.

My mother, filled with the Holy Spirit, reflected God's heart toward me that morning. The lie of shame and guilt no longer held me hostage. That day the gospel took on flesh in my life. My understanding of Jesus transformed from the image of a disapproving God into a loving Shepherd who sympathized with my weakness.

He stretched out his hand, accepted my brokenness, and promised to lead me, whether I was under a Mongolian sunset, in a suburban Wisconsin church, or on whatever path lay ahead.

your turn

Read

1 John 1:5-10

Reflect

1. What tends to get in your way when it comes to spending time with God? (Consider both external and internal distractions.)

2. What is your biggest sin struggle right now? How is it holding you back from spending time with God?

Grow

1. Think through your day and determine when and where you can set aside some time to spend with God. This will look different for all of us, depending on our life stage, personality, and circumstances. The important thing is to make it a priority and guard it the way we would time with a treasured friend. Commit to spending time praying and reading the Bible each day this week, even if it's just for a few minutes at first.

2. Prayerfully consider who you can share your sin struggle with. Confess your struggle to that person as well as to the Lord, resting in the assurance that no sin is beyond the reach of his grace. If you're having trouble knowing where to begin, you may want to use the prayer below.

Pray

Dear Jesus, I confess today that I struggle with _____. I'm so sorry for my failure to love and obey you in this area. Please give me the courage to confess my sin to _____. Prepare the time and place for me to share my struggle honestly with them, and don't let me lose my nerve before then. Thank you for setting me free from guilt by dying for me on the cross! Thank you that I am covered by your blood and that I can approach your throne with confidence. Please don't let my sin keep me from coming to you. Help me to take this step forward in repentance and faith. Amen.

2

guilt and grace

When We Fail to Have a Quiet Time

THE CONFESSION I MADE TO my mother that morning was a tipping point for my faith. I exposed my failure, and the grace my mom showed me revealed the gospel to me in a whole new way. For the first time, I started to grasp the kindness of God for sinners like me. I saw how sin and guilt were keeping me away from Jesus and his forgiveness. When I stopped pretending and brought my brokenness to God, I was able to experience the true depth of his mercy.

A weight was lifted off my shoulders, and I was more determined than ever to keep a close and obedient relationship with Jesus. But this time I was motivated not by guilt but by a desperate *need* for him. I became more watchful about my weakness and more transparent with others about my struggles. It felt euphoric to finally have a clear conscience! I decided to pour my newfound excitement and energy into the spiritual discipline I most wanted to improve: my quiet time.

Though it was still an uphill battle to read the Bible and pray every day, I felt certain that my encounter with grace would automatically make Bible reading and prayer easier. At first, I was right. I dove right into my daily devotions with great eagerness and felt closer to God than ever. I would journal late into the night, wake early to spend uninterrupted time in the Word, and frequently kneel by my bed to pray through my many prayer lists.

Now that I was a teenager, a daily quiet time was no longer a mandatory part of my homeschool curriculum. However, that freedom didn't diminish the expectations I had of myself. My goals included reading the whole Bible in a year, praying for at least thirty minutes every day, and memorizing as many verses as my brain could hold. It was a high standard for a thirteen-year-old! But I had a brand-new zeal for Jesus, and I was determined to walk with him.

For the first few months after my confession, my devotional habits remained consistent. This achievement sent my spirit soaring, and I thought my quiet-time struggle was officially over! Yet as time went on, my life slipped back into a mundane rhythm. My spiritual fervor began to wane, and my quiet time started to lose its consistency. I began missing days here and there and skimming passages instead of studying them.

Eventually I abandoned all efforts to memorize Scripture. One day I woke up and realized it had been over a month since I'd spent time with Jesus.

I was horrified. Gone was the zeal that had once fueled my daily devotion, and in its place was a throbbing guilt over what I saw as a duty I was failing to perform.

Maintaining a daily quiet-time habit had made me feel safe and self-assured in my faith, but now that my discipline was faltering, I trembled in fear. Was I really a Christian? If it was such a battle for me to spend time with Jesus, was my faith genuine? Once again, I began to feel guilty—and like an utter failure.

Quiet-Time Failure

Any Christian who has attempted to spend time with Jesus consistently knows what it's like to fail. We open our

Morgan's Quiet-Time Story

I know that Jesus loves when I spend time with him, but I also know that he doesn't want me to be a rigid, religious rule follower. When I'm sick or in need of rest, I typically don't spend time in the Word. I know that my salvation is not dependent on reading the Word at the exact same time every single day. I balance that with discipline by getting back on track with my regular routine of spending time in the Word and prayer as soon as I feel better.

Bibles on January 1 with the best of intentions, only to run out of steam by February. There are as many things to sidetrack us as there are hours in a day: work, kids, friends, husband, roommates, health problems, household responsibilities, TV, phone, sleep, worries, to-do lists. Even if we manage to carve out space for quiet time, it's hard to turn off the internal noise. No wonder so many of us bristle when we hear the phrase "quiet time." The words remind us of a failed ideal, and we'd rather avoid the topic than be reminded of our failure.

Maybe part of the problem has to do with our expectations of what our time with Jesus should look like. We tend to give spiritual credibility to the woman who wakes up at five o'clock in the morning to read her Bible or the person who prays for an hour every day or the mother who journals while sitting in her perfectly situated nook. Although certain believers in certain seasons of life are able to achieve these ideals, the rest of us struggle with a vague feeling of guilt whenever we compare our feeble efforts with these pictures of modern sainthood. Deep down we're ashamed of our hasty Bible skimming and distracted prayers. We know there's more to the Christian walk than squeezing in a few words with God before nodding off to sleep every night, but we're not sure if we can expect much more from ourselves.

As someone who is very driven and achievement focused, I have always taken pride in my successes and drowned in shame over my failures. As I struggled to spend time with

Jesus as a teenager, I saw myself as the one solely responsible for having a close relationship with the Lord. Somewhere along the way, I lost sight of the fact that God's grace isn't just for salvation; it's also what makes us grow. So it's no surprise that my striving for an ideal quiet time became a recipe for guilt.

When I went for a week straight without missing my quiet time, my spirit soared. But when I missed a day or two (or ten), suddenly my very salvation came into question. I became overwhelmed by discouragement, and my only hope was to try harder the next day and pray that this time the habit would stick. My relationship with God became something I needed to personally master instead of something to deeply enjoy, and reading the Bible became obligation instead of worship.

I was mired in guilt-motivated quiet time, and I was sinking fast.

The Worst Motivator

The truth is, we *do* have big things to feel guilty about, and I don't just mean the little mistakes or occasional errors we sometimes slip into. Rather, I'm talking about huge, cosmic, earth-shattering guilt. Whether we realize it or not, every one of us has each committed acts of high treason against the God who made us. Instead of honoring him and thanking him, we've rejected his rightful rulership over our lives and made ourselves king in his place. We've acted arrogantly, rebelliously, and selfishly toward God, and we've harmed others along the way.

So there's a legitimate reason for us to feel guilty, because without grace, we *are* guilty. But thanks be to God for Jesus! Because of his sacrificial death, we can now experience God's full pardon and mercy. Not only have our past sins been forgiven, but so has every wrong we will ever commit. Because of Jesus, we are welcomed into God's heart and God's family, and we are given the Holy Spirit to live in us and guide us. Because of Jesus, we can live free from shame. While it was right for guilt to drive us to the Cross, the Cross is where our burden of guilt gets removed for good. Though we still struggle with sin and evil desires, the ultimate battle has already been won! For those who love Jesus, guilty is what we used to be; holy is what we are and what we are becoming.

This means there's no place for guilt when it comes to spending time with Jesus. If guilt is the driving force, we will end up reading the Bible and praying only to soothe our conscience rather than to connect with Christ. Spending time with Jesus is a relational activity, not a guilt-driven obligation. He doesn't want us to swim in shame for missing a Bible reading—he desires genuine, joy-filled communion with us. And for that to happen, we have to kick guilt to the curb.

But if guilt is not our driving force, how can we be motivated to establish a daily quiet time? This is where it's helpful to understand the difference between *having* to do something and *needing* to do something.

A Way of Life

The fact is, doing daily devotions is not actually a requirement or a religious obligation for Christians. In other words, it's not a "have to." However, it *is* a desperate need. Having to do something means you have no choice or flexibility in the matter. Needing to do something means you'll be worse off if you don't. Just as we need to brush our teeth, eat our vegetables, and move our bodies to be physically healthy, we need to read the Bible and pray to keep our walk with God healthy and strong. Of course, our growth is an act of grace on God's part; it's not something we accomplish on our own. But God tends to work when we show up with humble hearts, ready to be changed.

But even though God is full of grace, that doesn't mean we can coast through life without discipline or intentionality.

Bethany's Quiet-Time Story

As most people probably know, having a quiet time is hard! I've had life seasons when I have either been very consistent about quiet time or I didn't sit down for weeks to study the Bible. Recently I've learned that it's not about how we study the Bible or that we check it off our list for the day; it's about spending time with the God of the universe, who made a way for us to know him and be with him. I don't have to prove myself to him when reading the Bible. I see now that quiet times look different depending on what is happening each day. Some days I'm able to spend a longer time studying verses and seeing what they mean. Some days I read a verse or two, or I go for a walk and spend time talking to God. It's not meant to be perfect. The most important things are just being with God and enjoying his presence.

While false guilt is not a good motivator, there *is* a place for holy conviction. Guilt is the feeling of having done something wrong. Conviction, on the other hand, is holding to a firm belief. While guilt dwells on the wrong committed in the past, conviction involves choosing a new path for the future.

Perhaps the most significant difference between conviction and guilt is that although conviction may hurt like guilt sometimes, it doesn't leave us wallowing in shame. Instead, conviction shows us the path out. Conviction is necessary for spending regular time with Jesus. Without conviction, a daily quiet time will remain nice in theory but will never become a consistent routine.

If you find yourself always focused on how you've failed in your daily quiet time, then you're living in guilt mode. But if you're looking ahead to how you can create or improve your quiet time because you firmly believe it's a worthwhile habit, then you are living by conviction.

The details of what that obedience looks like, especially when it comes to Bible reading and prayer, are different for every believer and for different seasons of life. There's no list of rules in Scripture about how to do daily devotions. Rather, relationship with Jesus is *a way of life*. Communicating with God in prayer and seeking the truth in his Word isn't just an item on a to-do list; it's a road to follow. This means there's freedom for each of us to seek Jesus in the way that works best for our unique personalities and life circumstances. It

Relationship with Jesus is a way of life.

also allows us to be individually responsible for these rhythms without condemning those who do things differently.

The Greater Treasure

If you've ever tried to successfully change unhealthy eating habits, you know that the answer is not simply saying no to everything you ate before. To experience lasting change, you have to start by saying *yes* to foods that are better for you. The old choices need to be replaced by better ones. The same is true when it comes to having a quiet time, struggling against sin, and deepening our relationship with Christ.

> *Quiet time isn't just an item on a to-do list; it's a road to follow.*

All sin is an effort to find our ultimate fulfillment in a lesser source. Just as with healthy eating, it's much more difficult to free ourselves from sin by simply telling ourselves to stop sinning. For instance, instead of just telling ourselves, "Stop gossiping," we need to pursue something more beautiful, like using our words to encourage and speak truth to others. If all we're worried about is achieving the perfect quiet time every day, we're destined for failure.

Instead of trying hard to check all the right boxes, I've found it helpful to set a better vision. This new vision is of Jesus himself, not the quiet time.

As we keep our eyes fixed on Jesus, it becomes easier to say no to what can never satisfy us (sin) and yes to the abundant life he offers. This is the *why* and *how* behind a quiet time. As we continue to practice the regular reading of God's Word and conversing with Jesus in prayer, we will find that our wandering hearts become more caught up with and tied to him, and less captivated by the idolatrous loves of this world. This is why we all desperately *need* daily time in the presence of Jesus!

Daily quiet time is simply a method by which we turn our eyes away from the things of this world and onto Christ. Don't make quiet time more than this! When we buy into the idea that the only way to appease God is by reading the Bible every day at six in the morning or praying through a long list of requests or spending an hour journaling in a beautiful prayer corner, we will be fueled by guilt instead of grace and we'll eventually be driven away from the Lord. But when we look at nothing and no one other than Christ, all our Bible-reading goals and prayer lists find their purpose. They can be a means of freedom and connection, and we will no longer feel shame and guilt when we aren't as consistent as we want to be.

Victory in the Effort

True success in quiet time is not about never missing a day but in coming back again tomorrow. There is victory in the effort itself. The danger comes when we give in to guilt and let shame take charge. It's the gospel that redeemed us in the first place, and it's the gospel we continue to need every day as we walk with him.

True success in quiet time is not about never missing a day but in coming back again tomorrow.

When we continue to struggle, there is hope. Over time, as we seek the Lord through prayer and his Word, we will be able to look back and see that our crying out to God has resulted in genuine spiritual growth. Eventually, quiet time will transform from a burden of duty into a cup of grace—a cup we can use to drink deeply from the Well of Life.

When our habits are based in grace, shame no longer has power over us. We are free to miss days here and there while still striving for overall consistency. Grace gives us a chance to breathe, embrace the gospel, and remember the reason we're reading the Bible and praying in the first place: to come face-to-face with Jesus.

your turn

Read

Romans 7:21–8:4

Reflect

1. In what ways is guilt keeping you away from Jesus? Read Romans 8:31-34 to find out what God's Word says about this kind of false guilt.

2. What convictions do you have when it comes to your quiet time? Are there any convictions you've been ignoring?

Grow

1. Write down the reasons you want to have a quiet time. Which of these reasons are based in guilt, and which are based in grace and conviction? Put a star by your grace-based convictions and cross out any guilt-driven reasons.

Pray

Dear Jesus, thank you that reading the Bible and praying are not in the category of "have to" for my salvation but "need to" for my spiritual health. Help me reject unnecessary guilt and live in the freedom of conviction. Please give me the grace to create and maintain a daily quiet time, and don't let guilt or shame keep me from coming to your merciful Cross. May *you* be the reason I build this habit, and may quiet time itself not be the end goal. Become my greatest treasure and my dearest delight. Amen.

drudgery, discipline, and delight

The Emotional Stages of a Quiet Time

IT WAS THE SPRING OF my fifteenth year, and life was going along as usual at the Straw Bale House. The days were filled with sunshine and trips to the nearby hills, where we would hike, pick edelweiss, and watch the countryside come back to life after the long, cold winter. We threw the windows of the Straw Bale House open, welcoming the warm breeze and the smell of dandelions. Life felt peaceful, predictable, and secure.

I had also settled into a fairly consistent spiritual routine. I was having regular quiet times, and my relationship with God was thriving. I was learning to embrace grace and say no to guilt. The future looked bright, with nothing to threaten the status quo.

Then my dad came home with news that upended my world.

After allowing us to stay in the Straw Bale House for more than ten years, the Mongolian family that owned the land was backing out of their agreement to let us live there. We would have to leave before the year ended.

I was devastated.

In one evening, my bright, secure world began to quake. Our family had lived in various places throughout my life, but the Straw Bale House had always been a fixture. This was where I'd spent my childhood and where I'd learned to read and ride a bike. It was where Jesus had met me during a sunset stroll. This place, built by my father and filled with precious childhood memories, had been an immovable sanctuary—a place where I could always return.

Now everything was about to change.

———

That summer we began to empty our closets and pack boxes full of kitchen supplies, clothing, and photo albums. Precious items were carefully wrapped in preparation for their next home, wherever that might be. I took slow walks around the yard every day, looking at the scraggly trees my mother had planted around the property, trying to imprint their outlines and colors in my memory before saying goodbye.

As we made plans to leave, the question looming in our

minds was where we would end up living. We considered moving farther out of town but ultimately decided this was a good time to be closer to our school friends in the city. Then my dad came up with an idea: What if we lived in the business building he managed, which was about a mile east of the city center?

This building, called Bubbling Springs, had been the hub of our social lives for many years. Not only was it where my dad worked every day, but it was also where our Mongolian church met on Sundays and where our international home-school co-op gathered on weekdays. It was a two-story building with a basement, surrounded by a bright red fence. There was a small fountain near the front steps that worked occasionally—and only during the few warm months of the year.

We all agreed that moving to Bubbling Springs was the right decision. After my dad did some renovation work, a portion of the second floor of Bubbling Springs would become our new home.

We continued to prepare for the move, both practically and emotionally. I found my once neat and orderly life slowly spiraling out of control. Meanwhile, so did my spiritual routines. Whenever I read my Bible, I got fidgety with worry, and I started shedding tears every time I prayed. Where I'd once felt steady and mature, I was now overcome with anxiety about the future. What would life look like in the city? Would I ever feel at home again?

Goodbye

The day of our departure finally arrived. Our friends showed up to help us pack, and we filled their cars with boxes, furniture, and miscellaneous items. Eventually the Straw Bale House stood empty, devoid of the objects, smells, and colors that had once brought it to life.

As the packing commotion swirled around me, I took a moment to stand in the doorway of each room, letting my mind's eye play back memories from the past ten years. The air seemed to hang heavily inside the empty rooms, and even the walls felt like they were watching me, wide eyed and bare. The windows were now tightly closed, their work of shielding us from winter storms and summer dust now complete.

I let my eyes rest on every crack in the wall and every piece of straw poking out of the ceiling boards. I knew each paint smudge, furniture dent, and crooked line in this house. There was the door that had held my third-grade reading chart. Next to it was the deep windowsill where I'd curl up and watch the rain. There was the spot where we would stand to warm our legs in front of the fire and the place where we'd blow out the candles and play hide-and-seek when the electricity went out. Peeking behind every corner were countless memories—moments that had filled my childhood with richness and joy.

I made my way into the yard next, knowing our departure was quickly approaching. I let my gaze linger on the spot where our garden used to be and where we once had a chicken coop. Then I looked at the old woodshed, where many secret meetings with my siblings had transpired, treasures had been stored, and eight puppies had been born on a summer night.

The emotions twisting inside me were raw and overpowering, unlike anything I'd felt before. No goodbye before this one had been so final. I knew everything would change once we started driving away, and I didn't know how to turn my back on this place.

But like it or not, the time had come. We piled into cars, and the rusty metal gate swung closed behind us for the final time. Tears ran down my face as I watched the chimney of the Straw Bale House fade into the distance. Eventually I turned around, trying to face the future that lay in front of me.

Lisa's Quiet-Time Story

Sometimes I feel that my quiet time isn't good enough or pleasing enough to God. On Instagram you see people talking about their quiet times, and they seem to be doing so much better than I am. But I'm learning that God made each of us unique and we all do things our own way. I used to feel terrible when I missed a day of quiet time, and then it would kind of snowball and turn into another day of not spending time with God. But I'm learning that God understands. We just have to do the best we can and trust that the Lord will lift us up. All we need to do is simply come, whatever way that works for us.

Made to Feel Deeply

There are few things as unpredictable as human emotion.

As a fifteen-year-old, I was just beginning to experience the ebb and flow of teenage hormones, so going through an unexpected move only magnified the onslaught of emotions. I found myself caught between the thrill of facing a new adventure and grief over the loss of my childhood home. One day I would be filled with an almost delirious excitement, and the next I would dissolve into tears of anguish.

These emotions also left their mark on my spiritual routines. Although I was beginning to understand the difference between guilt and conviction, my quiet times tended to ride the tide of my unpredictable emotions. For several days at a time I'd feel too emotionally wrung out to read the Bible and pray. Then one day I'd wake up and feel so hungry for the presence of Jesus that nothing could keep me from my Bible. Despite my best efforts, my quiet time was tied to my mood.

———————

Now that I'm in my late twenties, I can look back and smile at the plight of my younger self. I thought I was feeling a lot as a teenager. Little did I know just how many emotional ups and downs come with adulthood.

As humans, we are wired to feel emotions—and to feel them deeply. Whether we are rocked by a big life change or a move or unpredictable hormone levels, feelings are part of the territory. Emotions are a natural part of the way God has wired us, and they often serve as an indication of the state of our hearts. Feelings themselves aren't a bad thing; in fact, they can be a gift. However, things get complicated when those feelings sit in the driver's seat. In my own life, I've found that one of the greatest deterrents to spending regular time with Jesus is unpredictable emotions.

Maybe you've experienced something like this too. One day you wake up feeling content and excited to read God's Word, but the next day it suddenly seems like a task you dread for reasons you can't even explain. That's why it's so easy to slip into only having a quiet time when we feel like it. If our feelings are guiding us, our desires probably won't be consistent enough to establish this spiritual habit.

Many of us struggle because we believe the misconception that having a quiet time should make us feel a certain way. We expect that reading the Bible should give us an immediate dose of joy or that prayer should make us feel instantly connected to Jesus. Then when we experience anything less than these euphoric emotions, we assume that we aren't doing quiet time right. This mindset ignores the fickleness of human emotions and how much our habits and routines are affected by the feelings dancing around in our hearts. Yes, it's true that God created our feelings. But he should also be Lord over our feelings.

If you've practiced the habit of having a quiet time for several years, you've probably experienced a variety of emotional stages along the way. When we're new to the faith and full of zeal, reading the Bible and praying may feel effortless. As time goes by, however, spending time with Jesus might seem boring and even unenjoyable. When we feel this way, it's easy to become discouraged. We might be haunted by the question *Am I less in love with Jesus now than I was when I first became a Christian?* Or, *Why don't I feel the same way I did after summer camp or after that women's conference?*

When these struggles creep in, we may be tempted to slip away from our devotional routine. The truth is, though, if we keep pushing through these struggles, something much more meaningful—and enjoyable—awaits us.

The Three Emotional Stages of a Quiet Time

When we moved into our new apartment in the city, I thought I would never feel happy or at home again. It wasn't long until the initial thrill wore off, leaving me with a sense of gloom. I found myself trapped in a season of grief over the loss of the home we'd left behind. The idea that things would ever be normal again seemed impossible to believe.

At the time, I didn't realize I was experiencing the normal stages of emotions people face when encountering a big change. When we face significant transitions, our quiet-time habit (if we have one) often feels disrupted, even a drudgery. But if we persevere through this difficult season, spending time with God will eventually become an expected part of our day and routine. If we keep at it,

pressing forward in discipline, we will eventually experience the sweetest season of all: when time spent with Jesus
becomes a true delight.

These are the quiet-time stages, or seasons, which I refer
to as *drudgery, discipline,* and *delight.*[2]

Our new apartment was surrounded by concrete buildings,
without any horizon for me to watch my beloved Mongolian
sunsets. In this new environment, my country-loving heart
was covered by a dark cloud. I was staring at the first stage of
my emotional transition: the season of drudgery.

Drudgery

I could barely sleep the first night in our new apartment.

The night air never fell silent in the city. As I tried to get
comfortable, all I could hear were the sounds of drunken
people fighting, distant sirens blaring, and bad karaoke echo-
ing between the buildings. As the lights from a nearby apartment building streamed through my scant curtains, my eyes
remained wide open.

That first night I gave up on getting any sleep. Instead, I
got out of bed to creep over to my window. From the shadows I saw a man leave the bar next door and stumble past a
group of teenage boys, who stood smoking in a stairwell. A
woman in high-heeled shoes walked past the young smok-
ers, gripping her purse before ducking into an apartment

building across the lot. If I looked hard enough, I could see into the internet cafe across the street. It held expressionless, glowing faces, illuminated by blue computer monitors.

"The city never sleeps," as the saying goes, and it certainly seemed to be true here. This place was so unlike the previous neighborhood I'd lived in, where the nighttime sounds were made of whispering wind and dogs barking at one another. My old home had its fair share of danger, but it was nothing like this new apartment, which felt exposed and vulnerable in the heart of the city.

Everything was new, strange, and frightening.

By the next morning, any excitement I'd felt about living in this new place dissolved into a vague panic. That sense of dread never seemed to leave my chest. As I tried to adjust to our new home, the smallest task took a huge amount of effort. Whether it was finding the best walking route to the grocery store or trying to sleep at night with the karaoke bar blaring and our radiator pipes hissing, it felt like there was always some energy-draining obstacle to face.

Thus began my season of drudgery. It invaded every part of my life, from sleepless nights to my morning quiet time. Though I dragged myself to the Word, there was little joy or eagerness driving me. During prayer, my words were disjointed and distracted. What had once been a simple, happy habit turned into something akin to a school assignment. Why had my former zeal vanished? I missed the Straw Bale House, where I'd enjoyed a large yard to walk and pray through, a landscape of hills that sparked my soul, and a never-ending sky that reminded me of God's greatness.

Now what did I have?

We will all face seasons of drudgery and difficulty at some point as we attempt to establish or reestablish a regular quiet-time habit. Times of drudgery can be brought on by challenging circumstances, relationship difficulties, health problems, a life change, or simply the lull of the mundane. All at once our time with Jesus requires more energy than before, and there seems to be little fruit for our labor.

Seasons of drudgery expose what we previously relied on to feel "successful" in our spiritual routines. Before I moved, my life consisted of a wide-open sky, nearby hills, and a large yard. These good gifts had given breath to my time with the Lord and had created deep joy and

Hannah's Quiet-Time Story

Over the past three years of practicing quiet time, I've had seasons of consistency and times of inconsistency. Sometimes I feel discouraged when praying, and sometimes reading the Word seems mechanical to me, but God has been very kind toward me in my struggles, and he is transforming my heart. I know he wants us to know him intimately, and we can't wait until we feel motivated or inspired to spend time with him. Apart from Jesus, we can do nothing, so spending time in his presence is our lifeline.

delight. After these were taken away, I found it difficult to connect with God. My spiritual disciplines were stripped down to the basics: just me, my Bible, and the Lord.

What I didn't realize at the time was that I was going through a normal phase. My struggle wasn't a symptom of sin or spiritual sickness but rather a natural response to a difficult change. As universal as this experience is, however, there is a spiritual danger during seasons of drudgery. It's easy to give up when the going gets tough, and we may allow our hearts to drift away from Christ. When our hearts are left to wander, they are not in a neutral state. There are a host of outside influences and inward temptations that try to convince us that some other source can satisfy us better than Christ.

When I'm in a season of drudgery, my tendency is to turn inward and become complacent. In an attempt to feel happy again and break out of my lull, I go straight to what feels more exciting. This might mean jumping right into my workday as soon as the sun rises or popping on Netflix for hours on end. But inevitably, these habits never deliver on their promise of rest. Instead of feeling refreshed, I become more irritable, discontented, and thirsty. That's because no amount of temporary excitement can do for our souls what God and his Word can, whether we feel the effects immediately or not.

This is when it helps to remember that quiet time is not a "have to" but a "need to." So my motivation for having a quiet time instead of watching Netflix isn't because it's a religious obligation or something I have to do to get on God's good side; it's something I do because I really need him to speak into my life on a daily basis. TV shows and movies may be temporarily distracting, but they won't meet my deepest need, which is to know and enjoy and be changed by my Creator. Busying myself with work I enjoy might get my mind off my current difficulties for a little while, but it will do nothing to shift my gaze from earth to sky.

When we consistently spend time with the Lord, our gaze shifts from earth to sky.

Of course, it's not wrong to read a good book or watch a show occasionally. But if it becomes a pattern to choose these activities over spending time with the Lord, our closeness with God will suffer and our spiritual health will be stunted. This is why it's so important to keep pushing through the bog of drudgery to maintain a consistent relationship with Jesus. The best way to do this is to simply keep coming to him. Keep reading your Bible and keep praying, even when it seems unenjoyable or frustrating.

Similarly, in any marriage or friendship, there will be times when we are intentional about showing up in the relationship, whether the feelings are there or not. For example, my husband and I make it a point to sit down and ask each other specific questions about how we're doing every week. Sometimes it feels a bit like drudgery to stop everything else and talk through probing questions, but I've come to realize that without this intentional time together, Matt and I quickly become disconnected. Sticking to this routine helps our relationship thrive.

There is a simple truth we can cling to during the stage

of drudgery: it won't last forever. The beautiful thing about seasons is that they change, and when they do, we will never regret the times we persevered.

Discipline

City life was now my new normal.

Several months had passed since our move to the Bubbling Springs apartment. Our boxes full of clothes and dishes had new homes in their proper cabinets. The thin curtains that once hung in my bedroom had been replaced with heavier versions, and my walls now displayed artwork that made the room feel like my own. Night noises became less frightening, and the daily tasks of life became less intimidating.

What had once been a strange, scary place in the city had now become our home, and with that came a sense of routine. I no longer thought twice about which path to take to the market or woke up startled by the sounds of our radiators pinging strange notes. The school year was well underway, and as the temperature dropped, our entryway began to fill up with coats and boots. We'd brought along our woodburning stove to supplement the centralized city heat, which often left apartment dwellers wearing their coats inside. As the days grew shorter, darker, and colder, we spent more evenings in front of a crackling fire.

Though I was feeling more settled, I was still slightly numb emotionally. Since the drudgery and panic from our initial move had subsided, I now felt just okay. Not bad, but not great either. Daily life had settled into a predictable, ordinary rhythm, and so had my quiet time. My quiet time was no longer in a season of drudgery but a season of discipline. In the mornings I would roll out of bed, grab a cup of coffee from the pot my mom had already brewed, and find a quiet place to read the Word.

Although I was grateful it was no longer such a struggle to make these moments happen, it bothered me that much of my routine felt like going through the motions. But I decided it was better to go through the motions than to have no quiet time at all, so on I went, making my way through my reading plan, journaling, and praying as honestly as I could. It was a time of repetition, a time to be disciplined. Though my quiet time lacked the luster it once possessed, spending time with the Lord soon became a regular part of my daily routine.

In the season of discipline, you may still feel like you're simply putting one foot in front of the other, but quiet time will feel less difficult than before. If you persevere through the drudgery long enough, you'll discover that the season of discipline inevitably arrives.

Initially, this phase may seem alarming because it lacks emotion. You may even struggle with feeling like a hypocrite: there you are, reading your Bible and praying, but you're not feeling a genuine connection with Jesus. Instead of being dismayed, be encouraged! The season of discipline is normal, and sometimes routines will be just that: routine.

Just like with any worthwhile habit, there can be great benefit to going through the motions. It's valuable to maintain certain disciplines, regardless of how they make us feel. Things like brushing our teeth, going on a walk, or attending church are all healthy routines, and after a while, they become such natural parts of our lives that it would seem strange for a day to go by without them. Yes, there will be days when we deviate from our typical routines, but we usually come back to them, knowing that they're best for us.

It's worth noting that sometimes a lack of emotion indicates a deeper spiritual issue, such as unrepentant sin, discord in a relationship, or an inaccurate view of God, any of which could drain us of joy. The remedy is to keep spending time with the Lord, trusting that he'll help us through whatever the trouble is. Most often though, the dull feelings associated with a season of discipline are simply part of the ebb and flow of quiet-time stages.

Discipline itself is not the goal of quiet time. Jesus is.

While there's merit in developing a consistent rhythm, discipline itself is not the goal of quiet time. The point isn't just to read through the Bible in a year or pray through your entire prayer list every day. These activities are only tools that help us on our way to our ultimate goal: Jesus himself.

Delight

Finally, our first winter in the city was over. The ice had melted into mud, and the mud had given way to grass. The coal smog that smothered Ulaanbaatar had lifted, replaced by clear blue skies and brilliant sunlight. Dandelions were popping up along street corners and curbsides as daylight glowed far past our bedtimes and shone again hours before we crawled out of bed in the morning. Summer had finally arrived!

I was sitting on the front steps of Bubbling Springs, soaking in the warm sun. Two or three Mongolian children were playing in the fountain my dad had gotten running for the summer. It wouldn't be long before all the water activities, including water fights among the kids and clothes washing by homeless people in the area, would cause our fountain to clog up again. It felt like an absolutely perfect day.

Along with the arrival of summer came a feeling I thought I'd never experience again: delight. Gone was the drudgery that accompanied me when we first moved into our new apartment. Also gone was the sense of numbness that had stretched on for months. School was about to finish for the year, which meant that my friends and I would soon be playing street soccer and our own version of American baseball in a dilapidated stadium on a nearby hill.

It felt miraculous that this place that had once seemed so strange and unsafe now felt like home. I knew every shortcut, every knock-off brand clothing store, and every place I could get my favorite Mongolian foods for a cheap price. I learned that the row of benches along the sidewalk across from our building was where new mothers would bring their infants outside, all wrapped up in blankets. These women would sit, rocking their babies and visiting with other mothers and grandmothers for hours, no matter how cold it happened to be. I learned that the store across the street welcomed each new day with a loud blare of traditional Mongolian songs on their outdoor speaker system. At night, I no longer minded the off-key karaoke that boomed from restaurants and bars all around us, and each night I would eventually fall into a peaceful sleep to the discordant sounds. Wonder of wonders, I had actually come to enjoy the city.

I was experiencing the benefits of perseverance. Though this season of delight had come slowly and unexpectedly, it was finally here. No single event announced its arrival; it snuck in after days and weeks and months. In the midst of my seasons of drudgery and discipline, I found it hard to imagine that a time full of joy was right around the corner. But sure enough, it arrived, and as my life in the city became enjoyable, my time with the Lord also recovered its shine.

My daily quiet times were once again rich and full of enjoyment. Gone were the days of toil and monotonous routine! Now the words in my Bible sprang back to life, and Jesus seemed to be sitting across from me as I knelt in my sunlit bedroom. I couldn't get enough of him, and my heart overflowed with thankfulness as I experienced the rich connection I thought I'd lost, forever buried at the old

Straw Bale House. This was the season I'd been hoping for: a season of delight.

―――――――

Delight is by far the most enjoyable phase of having a consistent quiet time. It's the turning of the page we long for when we're in the midst of more difficult spells. In this time of delight, the Word of God glows again, our prayers flow effortlessly, and our connection to Jesus feels deep and full. Just as I was seeing my city home with more appreciation, my eyes were opened anew to the beauty and love of our Father, and my heart couldn't help but respond with shouts of joy.

You might wonder if this stage of delight even exists. Maybe you've been trudging through the phases of drudgery and discipline for so long that these green pastures and quiet waters seem like a mirage or a distant memory. Take heart, fellow pilgrim. It really is possible to experience delight in the presence of God.

It helps to remember that there's nothing we can do to earn or force ourselves into a season of delight. We can, however, ask our Father to lead us into those lush green pastures, since God is the Shepherd of our seasons. If we persist in seeking him, a greater delight will surely follow. As we intentionally practice giving thanks always, praying unceasingly, and rejoicing in every circumstance (even when we don't feel very joyful), we'll soon find the ice around our hearts melting, giving way to a sense of jubilee.

The key is to persevere. Keep seeking God, even through feelings of discouragement and doubt. Keep reading the Bible, even when picking up your Bible is the last thing you want to do. Keep praying, even when your prayers feel dry and dusty and broken. At times like these, we may wonder, *Is Christ really worthy of being pursued as our ultimate treasure?* Yes, he is! Jesus is worthy of being pursued, no matter how we feel. The delight of an intimate relationship with him is worth striving toward and waiting for.

Jesus is worthy of being pursued, no matter how we feel.

Although it's possible to experience passing glimpses of delight without a regular quiet-time habit, nothing can compare to the deeper joy that comes with establishing regular Bible reading and prayer. Instead of tasting bits and pieces of God's Word, we will have a foundational understanding to pull insight and wisdom from. Instead of approaching Jesus like strangers, we can gain the familiarity of speaking with him as a close friend who already knows the details and depths of our hearts. Sporadic, impulsive moments of prayer will never compare to the delight produced by faithful prayer and time in his Word.

Once you have persevered through the valley of drudgery and the desert of discipline, the season of delight will feel like the arrival of a cool summer rain. It may take weeks, months, or even years before we find ourselves arriving at last to the season of delight, but when we do, we will discover that all the waiting and persevering was worth it. Like grace itself, delight in the presence of God is not a reward we earn but a gift we receive! In the season of delight, there's nothing more to be done than to drink deeply and enjoy Jesus, our treasure. This is what God desires for us, since we bring glory to God best when we enjoy him most.

Feelings Change, but God Stays the Same

The stages of drudgery, discipline, and delight are not linear; they are cyclical. I used to think that I would only have to walk through drudgery one time and that once I reached delight, I would be set for the rest of my life. But that's not how seasons work. Suffering will come, transitions and emotional changes will catch us off guard, and all at once we will find ourselves relearning what it means to seek the Lord in different seasons.

Even as we mature in our faith, we won't do quiet time perfectly. Sometimes in a season of drudgery, we'll be distracted from the Lord, or during a season of discipline, our hearts will be lulled into complacency. Even during times of delight, we may be tempted by pride. When these things happen, let's remember once again the kindness, mercy, and grace God has shown us through Jesus. It's Jesus who saves and changes us. He understands and is sympathetic to our emotional ups and downs. When we are inconsistent, his love for us doesn't change. Nothing, not even our own failures, can keep his love away from us.

Nothing, not even our own failures, can keep God's love away from us.

Although our emotions fluctuate,

God's feelings about us don't change. Times of drudgery don't mean he is angry with us, times of discipline don't mean he is distant, and seasons of delight don't mean we've done anything to deserve them.

Feelings are created by God, and when they're kept in their rightful place, they're a gift. Our emotions reflect the deep recesses of our hearts, and they allow us to genuinely connect with others who are walking through similar seasons. However, our feelings must not take the place of objective truth and God's authority. What we know of God through his Word must transcend all sentiments, and as we are faithful to trust and obey, our feelings will eventually follow. God wants us to experience the deepest, richest, most lasting happiness possible, and he won't allow us to settle for temporary fixes and empty delights that will ultimately disappoint us.

This means you can trust God with your feelings. He is a Good Shepherd, and he won't lead you astray. Resolve now to endure through the stages of quiet time, knowing that all your effort and patience will be worthwhile—in this life and for eternity.

Lasting delight is waiting for you at the foot of the Cross.

your turn

Read

Proverbs 3:5-6; Philippians 3:12-21

Reflect

1. What are some recent transitions you've experienced? How did these transitions make you feel? How did they affect your quiet time?

2. How do you feel about your relationship with God and having a quiet time right now? Are you in a season of drudgery, discipline, or delight?

Grow

1. If you are in a season of drudgery, consider simplifying your quiet time to make it as easy as possible. The main goal right now is to just show up! If you are in a season of discipline, try adding a new element to your quiet time that could help spark your delight. (See chapter 7 for some ideas.) If you are in a season of delight, enjoy!

Pray

Dear Jesus, thank you for being a God who feels emotion and for creating me to have feelings. I surrender all my emotions to you today. I am currently in a season of _____. Please take this stage of my life and work it together for my good and your glory.

Help me to continue seeking you, even when I don't feel like it. Give me perseverance in times of drudgery, joy in times of discipline, and humility and gratitude in times of delight. Amen.

4

the most important habit

Making Jesus Part of Our Everyday Lives

THE PLANE WAS DARK AND FULL of sleeping passengers.

The hum of the engine and the dim lights created a perfect atmosphere for napping, but after ten hours in the air, it was getting harder to find a comfortable position. I looked over and saw my mom, glasses on and book in hand as we made our way across the Pacific Ocean. It was just her and me this time.

I was eighteen years old and moving to America for good.

My body and soul were exhausted from all the emotions of the past few months. I'd graduated high school only to discover that my Mongolian visa wouldn't allow me to stay in the country as an eighteen-year-old. Although I knew I would have to leave my homeland one day, this eviction felt stark and sudden.

The leaving process was a whirlwind of planning, praying, and saying heart-wrenching goodbyes. I spent my last days in Mongolia sorting through my belongings, trying to fit most of my possessions into two suitcases, and visiting as many of my favorite childhood spots as possible.

The night of my departure arrived all too quickly. My mom and I were taken to the Mongolian airport by family and friends, who waved goodbye from the other side of the glass until we disappeared behind the security gate. My mom and I boarded the plane at midnight, and after buckling my seat belt, I melted into my oversized hoodie and cried.

Twenty hours later, we were on the second-to-last leg of our journey. The last stop would be a small city in Central Florida. A Christian family there had offered me a place to stay as I made the transition from life overseas. I'd initially turned down their offer, since I saw Florida as nothing more than a glorified swamp. Heat, humidity, and large insects were not my idea of a good time. However, I had to go somewhere, and after wrestling with the decision in prayer, I felt certain that the Holy Spirit was leading me to Florida. So there I was, hugging my travel pillow in a cramped airplane seat as nearly everything I knew and loved faded away at the speed of five hundred miles per hour. With what seemed like an eternity of plane rides, vacuum-sealed food trays, and crowded terminals, we finally arrived, plane-scented and bedraggled, at Tampa International Airport.

My new host family was waiting at the terminal, and they welcomed me with smiles and hugs. Their warm embrace gave my insecure heart just the comfort it needed to know that everything was going to be okay. The air outside was just as hot as I imagined it would be, but as we drove away from the airport, I found myself transfixed by the slender palm trees that lined the highway.

An hour later, we pulled into my host family's neighborhood, and the beauty of the scene took my breath away. The grass was greener and thicker than any I'd ever seen, the houses stood tall and stately, and even the sidewalks sparkled. Awe set in as I toured what was to be my new home. I'd never lived in a place as nice as this one, and I couldn't quite wrap my mind around the luxuries of two stories and a pool.

The first few days passed quickly as I unpacked my suitcases and got to know my host

Sarah's Quiet-Time Story

Having quiet time with Jesus honestly changes the whole trajectory of my day. Whether it's early in the morning before work or right before I go to bed, I feel at peace and comforted by the guiding words of Scripture. The way I view others, handle situations, make decisions, and choose my words is often based on whether I started off the day spending time with God, asking him to be my hands and feet and to give me his supernatural grace, forgiveness, kindness, and understanding. Quiet time allows me to reflect on how I am ultimately reflecting the heart of Jesus throughout my day.

family. With my mother close by, I felt confident, maybe even a little cocky, that I'd be able to transition into this new American life. However, she didn't stay long, and I was only just getting used to the thirteen-hour time difference when it was time for her to return to Mongolia. As I watched her disappear into the airport terminal, doubt began to trickle in. The last tie to my former life was walking away, and I was on my own.

It suddenly occurred to me that I knew absolutely nothing about living in America. I would need to learn how to drive a car, use American money, shop for groceries, and find some kind of job. Even my wardrobe was incompatible with this climate. I only knew how to dress in layers, and I felt uncomfortable showing my legs or shoulders in public. My blood had been thickened from years of living in Siberia, and there were days when not even the air-conditioning of my host family's house was enough to cool me down. Sometimes the only thing I could do to experience relief was stick my head in the kitchen freezer.

I was going to have to relearn every rhythm I'd created, every routine I'd developed, everything I thought I knew about life. The prospect was exhausting.

Thankfully, God's grace was waiting for me. Only he can turn the foreign into familiar and the exhausting into ordinary.

The Necessity of Habit

The first challenge was learning how to drive a car.

A driver's license would be necessary for me to function as

an adult in the US, so with the help of my host parents, I got behind the wheel. I'll never forget putting my foot on the gas pedal for the first time. Utter terror would be an understatement. I had to focus with my entire mind on every little task, from buckling my seat belt to adjusting my mirrors to putting my hands on the steering wheel at ten o'clock and two o'clock. Every turn was terrifying and every stoplight induced panic, and after each trip around the neighborhood, I would emerge trembling from the driver's seat and collapse on the couch.

I know I'm not the only one who has experienced the nerves that come with undertaking something new. Learning any skill is overwhelming at first for the simple reason that we've never done it before. Our brains love the ease of rhythm and repetition, so whenever we're introduced to something new, our minds have to focus all our energy on adopting the unfamiliar skill set. No wonder I was so exhausted during the first several months of living in America! Every task was brand new, from learning to drive to using American currency to choosing an outfit each morning.

It's not necessary to move to another country to experience this struggle. Learning a new routine or changing an old one can quickly tire us out, whether it's a way of eating, a workout program, or simply trying to get up an hour earlier every day. For a while, any unfamiliar task is incredibly demanding, and that's true not only physically and mentally, but spiritually too. The same goes for reading the Bible: if you're not used to having a regular quiet time, this new habit will require a lot of intentional focus. If you're not used to praying, it's easy to feel overwhelmed.

Or maybe you're the kind of person who finds it exciting and motivating to start something new, like the little thrill when you sit behind the wheel of a car for the first time. As an ambitious person, I tend to find myself adopting a "go big or go home" mindset, setting huge Scripture-reading and journaling goals. But after the initial buzz wears off, I realize this unfamiliar routine requires more energy and focus than I thought possible. This is when it's easy to become inconsistent with quiet time or give up on it altogether. It takes a lot of time and practice to turn the occasional dabble into a lasting habit.

The other day I got into my car and was out of my driveway and onto the road in less than a minute. I didn't even notice myself putting on my seat belt or looking both ways before pulling out. My mind was on other things, and before I knew it, I'd arrived at my destination. It's been ten years since I learned to drive, and all that practice has resulted in a habit that's now second nature. I like to refer to this as "the rule of habit," which simply means that the more you do something, the easier it gets.

Author Charles Duhigg has done extensive research on the human brain's ability to create habits. He explains why the brain operates this way in his book *The Power of Habit*:

Habits, scientists say, emerge because the brain is constantly looking for ways to save effort. Left to its own devices, the brain will try to make almost any routine into a habit, because habits allow our mind to ramp down more often. This effort-saving instinct is a huge advantage. . . . An efficient brain also allows us to stop thinking constantly about basic behaviors, such as walking and choosing what to eat, so we can devote mental energy to inventing spears, irrigation systems, and, eventually, airplanes and video games.[3]

This brain mechanism explains why it's so difficult to learn something new and so easy to do something we've done a thousand times. Our brains create neurological pathways when introduced to an unfamiliar concept, task, or routine. As we repeat the steps, these pathways are solidified into established habits. Habits are what take us from stumbling toddlers to functioning adults. God designed our brains to develop routine behaviors so we could conserve energy, learn higher-level skills, and go about our days without dying of exhaustion. That's the good news.

The bad news is that habits are also difficult to break. In order to learn something new, we have to unlearn a previous habit. That's why eating healthily is difficult when we're used to consuming fast food on the regular. It's why working out is hard when our bodies are used to relaxing. It's also why having a quiet time in the morning instead of jumping straight into work or scrolling social media can be such a struggle.

Thankfully, habits can and do change. With effort and practice, we can take one habit and turn it into another. However, in order for us to stick with the hard work of habit building, we must first be convinced that daily Bible reading and prayer is worth it. Why put in the effort to unlearn one routine and replace it with a new one? Because what we value most will inevitably be displayed in our daily habits. And there's nothing more valuable than our relationship with Jesus.

What we value most will inevitably be displayed in our daily habits.

The Habit of Relationship

Our habits reflect what we value.

If you value being clean, then you've probably developed the habits of showering and putting on deodorant. If you value looking presentable, then you've probably developed the habit of selecting outfits from your closet. If you value having a healthy body, then you've probably developed the habits of exercising regularly and eating nutritiously. Whether intentionally or unintentionally, we develop habits and routines that reflect what we value most. Either we make conscious choices about our habits, like waking up early or exercising, or we allow our cravings to determine our routines. Without exerting self-control over our habits, we'll end up eating ice cream for breakfast and watching TV all day.

As believers, we are, of course, eager to claim that our greatest treasure is Christ. But this is easier to talk about than to practice, particularly because there are so many values battling for our affections. Even though we *want* to want Jesus more than anything else, our wandering hearts are drawn to lesser things. It takes more effort to spend time with Christ than it does to watch a movie, read an entertaining book, or sleep for an extra hour. It goes against our sinful nature to enjoy Jesus more than we enjoy the good things he has created.

And if this inner battle isn't enough, we also have external influences that war against our quiet-time habit. Our culture bristles against the concept of self-discipline, and even some Christians don't want to box themselves into a spiritual routine. It's true that God desires a relationship with us, not just repetitious, religious routines. But can a relationship thrive without intentional routine? Every healthy, fulfilling relationship requires self-control, consistency, and intention. That's why it's so important to sift through our competing desires, resist our culture's misplaced priorities, and pursue a daily, intentional relationship with Christ. Of course, we don't want our quiet times to be the only times we pray, but if our conversations with God are based solely on impulse, we will soon discover that other habits and routines will crowd out our best intentions.

God never meant for our relationship with him to be made up entirely

> *God never meant for our relationship with him to be made up entirely of mountaintop experiences. He desires all of us.*

Until we decide to make our relationship with Jesus ordinary, we will miss out on the extraordinary.

of mountaintop experiences and emotional highs. Rather, he desires *all* of us—our schedules, friendships, possessions, and priorities. He wants us to experience the depths and riches of his love, but these treasures lie on the other side of consistent faithfulness. Until we decide to make our relationship with Jesus ordinary, we will miss out on the extraordinary. Unless we welcome him into our daily schedules, our lives will move on without him.

Making Quiet Time a Habit

When it comes to creating a new routine, having a plan is half the battle. We can't assume that a healthy relationship with Christ will just happen on its own. Although the strength of the relationship is based on God's power, not ours, the Bible won't find its way into our hands without a choice on our part. If we want to know Scripture better, pray more regularly, and deepen our daily walk with Jesus, then we must make a plan.

Here are some tips to begin the process of building a quiet-time habit.

Start Small

Many people make the mistake of getting too ambitious and complicated with their quiet time. If you make it your goal to study the Bible for an hour, journal, memorize Scripture, and then pray for another hour, you're probably not going to stick with it for very long! To give yourself the best fighting chance, start small. Five or ten minutes in the Lord's presence is better than none at all, and it will be easier to add more time after you've built up your quiet-time muscle.

To start out, focus on simply reading the Bible. You'll be able to study more in depth once your quiet-time habit is established, but for now, begin by reading small sections of Scripture. (If you're not sure where to start, use the Scripture references at the end of these chapters.) Use a Bible that's easy to understand and that you're not afraid to mess up and make notes in.

After that, spend a few minutes praying. You can pray silently or out loud, with your eyes open or closed—whatever feels most natural for you. Try thanking God for a few things, talking with him about something you're struggling with or a need you have, and then ending with a request for someone else.

Pick a Time Every Day

Quiet times can happen anytime, anywhere. However, if we want to create a habit, it helps to choose the same general time every day to help our subconscious minds register the routine. Mornings and evenings tend to stand out most in our minds, especially since these times are often associated with other routines. It's easier to have a consistent quiet time when we can tag it onto the end or the beginning of another routine that's already established, such as morning coffee or bedtime.

During some seasons of our lives, however, our morning and evening schedules are unpredictable. This is especially true for caregivers or mothers of young children or people with chronic health conditions. During challenging seasons like these, the best mindset may simply be survival. Maybe all you can manage is to pray while in the shower, meditate on Scripture while you nurse the baby, or sneak in ten minutes of Bible reading while the kids are napping. God's grace will meet you there, too.

Keep Your Bible on Your Nightstand

One habit that has helped me be more consistent with quiet time over the years is putting my Bible somewhere I see it often. This may seem silly, but the first thing our subconscious mind looks for when performing a routine is a cue to start the activity. If you keep your Bible in view, it keeps quiet time at the forefront of your mind. Better yet, open your Bible to the passage you're currently reading and place it on your nightstand or coffee table. You might even find yourself glancing at the words or picking it up to read more throughout the day. Do whatever it takes to make your quiet time as easy as possible—and as much a normal part of your day as possible.

Decide on a Bible Reading Plan

One of my biggest pet peeves is deciding what to watch on TV with my husband. It takes us at least fifteen minutes to scroll through our options and another fifteen minutes to actually make a decision! At times we get so frustrated with the decision-making process that we lose the desire to watch TV at all.

One of the biggest drains on our energy is decision making. So if you start your quiet time not knowing what you're going to read next, you may tire out before you even get started. That's why it helps to keep things simple for yourself and choose a plan. (You can visit biblegateway.com or navigators .org/resource/bible-reading-plans for Bible reading plans.) That way all your energy can go toward actually reading.

Another benefit of having a Bible-reading plan is that it will take you through all of Scripture instead of just bits and pieces. The Bible is a story, not simply a collection of verses. Having a reading plan will help you travel through Scripture in its full context.

Rachelle's Quiet-Time Story

I struggle with anxiety, and fear is something I have to fight very hard against. I love Psalm 23, and especially verse 4: "Even when I walk through the darkest valley, I will not be afraid, for you are close beside me. Your rod and your staff protect and comfort me." I take comfort in the fact that I don't have to fight my fears alone. I can choose the comfort of the Lord over fear.

Create a Prayer List

Just like with Bible reading, it helps to have a plan to guide your prayers. The simplest way to do this is to create a list. We will talk more about prayer in chapter 6, but as you get started, you might want to write down a few things to pray about every day. I recommend including something you're thankful for, something you love about God, a need or want that someone else has, and a need or want that you have. This list can expand and change over time, and as you pray, you'll find yourself adding more items to talk about with Jesus. But for now, start small.

Choose a Spot

To help make your quiet time a habit, choose a specific place to have it every day. If you have a favorite chair or a peaceful spot in your home, use that space for your quiet time. As with choosing a reading plan, it takes less energy to have a quiet time if we already know where we're going. The more consistent we are with the details surrounding our quiet times, the more habitual the routine will become and the easier it will be to maintain.

Make It Something to Look Forward To

It may be cliché, but there's a reason coffee and quiet time have become a couple. If the routine is tied to something we find enjoyable and rewarding, a habit will form more quickly. This is why I believe it helps to surround ourselves with things that engage our senses. Do you have a front porch? Use it for your quiet time. Do you have a favorite blanket? Spread it over your lap before you begin. Do you have a scented candle you love? Light it while you pray. These little touches make daily devotions a more enjoyable experience, which will make it a habit more quickly.

We don't gain spiritual points for making our quiet time minimalistic and stark. God doesn't think more of us if we refuse to acknowledge anything other than the Bible page we're studying. Just as walking through a forest or on a beach can help us appreciate God's beauty, drinking a cup of coffee or lighting our favorite candle can help us feel closer to him during our quiet time. Of course, these accessories aren't required to spend time with Jesus, and they won't always be available to us, but we can appreciate them as gifts of common grace. The goal is to create an enjoyable system that will enable us to turn the routine of a quiet time into a lasting habit.

Habits of Grace

The question is not whether we will have habits, but which habits we will allow to take over our lives. They can either help us in our pursuit of Christ or keep us locked in complacency. There is nothing more rewarding and fulfilling than the habits that lead us to a real, intimate relationship with Jesus.

If you are finding a quiet-time habit difficult to establish, remember that all habits are hard to develop. Just because you struggle with daily devotions doesn't mean you are somehow less redeemed, holy, or capable than Christians who have a regular time with Jesus. It simply means that they've made this a habit. The good news is that it's possible to make Jesus part of our everyday schedule. When we do, we will discover the beauty of routine, the obedience of rhythm, and the extraordinary delight of bringing Jesus into our ordinary days.

your turn

Read

Psalm 1

Reflect

1. What habits make up your typical day?

2. What do your habits reveal about your values?

Grow

1. Write down a time and place you could have your daily quiet time.

2. Choose a Bible reading plan and start reading today!

3. Make a list of three to five things you can pray about, and then pray through your list.

Pray

Dear Jesus, thank you for designing our brains to adopt routines and create habits. Forgive me for my habits that don't please you, and by your grace, help me to change those habits. Help me not to neglect spending time with you. Give me the wisdom to know when, where, and how I should have a quiet time, and help me to persevere in this routine until it becomes a firmly fixed habit in my life. Amen.

5

reading the bible

Loving and Living God's Word

THE CAMPUS WAS A SEA OF skinny jeans and V-neck tees. I gripped my backpack as I wove through buildings and hallways toward my next class. Freshman year had just begun, and I found myself faced with another wave of culture shock, one that involved the unique subculture of a private Christian university.

I'd never seen so many self-professing Christians in one place. It was a requirement for the application process to profess faith, so every student on campus at least had a basic understanding of Christianity. Having lived in a country where I was a religious minority, I now felt practically dizzy over how easily people talked about Jesus. The experience was exhilarating . . . and confusing.

After living in a place where only a small number of other people claimed to follow Jesus, it felt disorienting to attend crowded chapel services, which included high-energy displays of lights, fog machines, and beautiful people yelling passionately for about ten minutes. One night, the band transitioned seamlessly from a worship song into "I Wanna Dance with Somebody (Who Loves Me)" by Whitney Houston. The college students who had been swaying and weeping with their hands lifted high now roared in delight as the worship leader crooned, "Oh! I wanna dance with somebody / I wanna feel the heat with somebody!" That's when I realized I had entered a strange land indeed—one where hype was high, entertainment was key, and worship services could transform into pop culture concerts in ten seconds or less.

As I settled into my classes, I realized I had more to worry about than unpredictable chapel services. While most of my teachers opened their classes with a brief word of prayer and a Bible verse or two, there were a couple of theology professors who seemed to make it their goal to rattle the faith of young students without giving much guidance afterward for picking up the pieces. It seemed as though not a single class went by without someone questioning the inerrancy of God's Word or casting the concepts of hell and moral absolutes in a skeptical light. While this way of thinking wasn't necessarily the position of the school, a handful of professors made my journey through college feel like a spiritual battleground.

Now I understood why my parents had insisted on teaching me Scripture. Instead of leaving my faith in the hands of Whitney Houston-inspired worship leaders or edgy professors, my parents knew I would need to rely on Scripture as my infallible guide. As I approached the door of my theology classroom each week, I was thankful I'd read and studied the Bible for myself. I knew that Scripture would provide me with more than just murky classroom intellectualisms; it was my source of absolute truth.

Why We Read the Bible

Unless we know what the Bible actually says, we are at risk of swallowing the opinions being fed to us. Without Scripture as our standard, we won't have the discernment we need to uncover the truth. Even if someone is a pastor or a professor at a Christian school, that doesn't mean they've tied themselves to the higher authority of Scripture. Just because someone

Jordan's Quiet-Time Story

I've had to learn to separate Bible reading from in-depth study. Both are good. Both have their time and place. But I've come to realize that each time I open my Bible I don't have to look up the author of each book, when it was written, and to whom it was written. I don't have to look up every definition to every word. I love this type of in-depth study, but I was missing out on prayer time and simple truths that didn't require all that work.

has been given a platform, that doesn't mean what they're saying is right. There is only one authority for all truth, one source that stands out from all the other voices, and that's God himself, revealed through his Word.

The only way we can tell the difference between accurate Bible teaching and human speculation is to have a firsthand understanding of God's Word. During my college years, I became even more passionate about reading the Bible every day, mainly because I became aware of how many voices were attempting to convince me of other perspectives. I needed to be grounded in eternal truth so I wouldn't be swept away by trendy teachings.

While there are many reasons for us to make Bible reading a regular part of our quiet time, there are three reasons that stand out.

The Bible Reveals Who God Is

People-watching is one of my favorite pastimes. As I observe strangers, I try to guess where they're from, what they do, and where they're going. This is especially fun in airport terminals, which are filled with travelers from all over the world. As I wait to board a flight, I often create stories about the people around me.

One time, after boarding a plane, I ended up sitting next to one of the people I'd been watching at the terminal gate. I had assumed he was an American businessman, but after speaking with him for a few minutes, it became clear that my earlier imaginings were way off! It turned out he was an artist from Germany! As he told me about his life, I was able to replace my far-off assumptions about him with a more accurate reality.

This is what happens when we actually get to know someone.

You can make any number of guesses about someone's character and nature, but unless they choose to reveal themselves to you, you'll be left with your own unfounded speculations. This is the primary reason we need to read and love the Bible: through it, God reveals himself to us!

On the pages of Scripture, we come to understand God's nature, his beauty, his desires, and his majesty. The Bible is a window into heaven itself—a trustworthy revelation of who God Almighty is.

The Bible Reveals Who We Are

Another one of my favorite pastimes is strolling through art galleries. The paintings and sculptures capture my attention, and I'm content to roam there for hours. However, I always find myself perplexed when I get to the modern-art section. The seemingly random lines and splashes of color leave me confused. What was the artist thinking?

That's when I lean in and read the title and description of the piece.

As I find out about the author's intent, the meaning of the art becomes clearer. The title may not clarify everything, and we may bring a facet of our own interpretation to the piece, but there's no denying that the artist had a specific vision for the work they created.

You and I are works of art too—masterpieces made by God with a specific design and meaning. No one besides our Creator can rightfully define who we are, what we are like, and what we're meant for. For this reason, the Bible is also our guide for understanding humankind, from the past epochs of history to the present depths of our own hearts.

The pages of Scripture reveal everything we need to know about our origin, our identity, our purpose in this world, and our destiny in the world to come. These questions about existence and our place in it have intrigued philosophers for thousands of years, and the answers are found in the pages of Scripture.

The Bible Reveals Reality

Every time I go to Ikea, I come back with something that contains a hundred tiny pieces and requires at least an hour to assemble. My husband and I have spent an incredible amount of time lining up pieces on the floor, searching for missing screws, and laboring over the "some assembly required" furniture we purchased the day before. If I've learned anything from these experiences, it's that every piece has a design and a function, and if you want to figure out how the proper pieces work together, you need to read the instructions.

Without the manual, a project that should take only a

couple of hours might become an all-day activity—and a frustrating one, at that. Furthermore, without access to these detailed instructions, the final result is a piece of furniture that doesn't work properly or even breaks. In order to successfully put together an item from Ikea, you must be aligned with the reality of the design.

The same is true when it comes to living in the world God designed. It's in the Bible that we discover what reality is and how we should function within it. Not only did God create humans for a specific function, but he also designed this whole world with great care and purpose. The Bible explains how this good design was broken when sin entered the picture. But we have not been left hopeless! The Bible also reveals Jesus, the one who can restore us and the world we live in. Thanks to Jesus, we can experience the original purpose God created us for.

The analogy isn't perfect though, because the Bible isn't really an instruction manual or a set of rules to follow so we can have a comfortable, problem-free life. Instead, the Bible is good news for messed-up, shame-filled, broken sinners. The Bible helps us understand how God meant for the world to work and how we can best live within that design until the restoration of all things (see Acts 3:21). In the pages of Scripture, we learn how to live, work, relate to others, worship God, enjoy creation, and handle any situation we might face. At its heart, the purpose of the

There is no more accurate guide to understanding reality than the Word of God.

Bible is to help sinful people find reconciliation with God and experience the restoration of God's design through the work of Jesus Christ.

There is no more accurate guide to understanding reality than the Word of God.

How to Read the Bible

I used to think that intensive Bible study was necessary for having a quiet time. I would pull out all my highlighters, commentaries, dictionaries, and Bible apps, only to give up in discouragement after having unsuccessfully wrestled through a passage for two hours. I did this based on the notion that what set a quality quiet time apart from a mediocre one was in-depth Bible study. The pressure from this expectation quickly became exhausting, leaving me discouraged and drained instead of fulfilled. In short, I'd made a certain way of studying the Bible a rule instead of a tool.

Of course, it's important to study the Bible—and to study it deeply and with great effort. God's Word deserves our utmost care and attention. However, the Bible is also worthy of being read line by line, chapter by chapter, and book by book. It's possible for God's Word to be savored without all the commentaries, highlighters, and hermeneutical processes that I used to think were necessary for an adequate quiet time. By God's grace, I eventually started to see the beauty of not just studying the Bible but also reading it simply for the pleasure of doing so.

Here's the basic difference between reading Scripture and studying it: we read the Bible to know what it says, and we study the Bible to better understand what it says. We need to do both! Our goal is to know and love God's Word, and that can be achieved during times of simple reading as well as times of in-depth study. The most important thing is that God's Word is central to our quiet time.

There are several ways to approach Bible reading: reading the Bible as a story, reading the Bible to see and experience Jesus, and reading the Bible to be changed.

Reading the Bible as a Story

In our sound-bite culture, it's common for Scripture to be treated like a collection of verses rather than as an overarching narrative. The Bible is viewed as a candy bag full of feel-good clichés you can reach into for a topical sermon, a political point, or a greeting card.

The truth is, the Bible isn't just a bunch of sayings meant to serve the reader's agenda. Rather, all of Scripture is a single, cohesive story with contextual threads that run from start to finish. Like any good story, it begins with a hero (God), a villain (sin and Satan), a damsel in distress (humanity), and a sorrowful tragedy (the Fall). In the pages that follow, we see how God, the hero, works to rescue and redeem the damsel in distress from her tragic state and restore all of creation back to himself. The only difference is that every word of this story is true.

The entire Bible was written as part of this bigger story, which means it doesn't make sense to focus on a handful of verses while ignoring the rest of Scripture. We may find some passages boring, uncomfortable, or offensive to our modern sensibilities, but every part of God's Word is there for a purpose. That's why it's helpful to use a Bible-reading plan that takes you through the entire Bible. The plan doesn't need to be completed within a year or even two, but it should eventually take you through every part of God's Word. Only then will you be able to see the bigger story at work within the pages of the Old and New Testaments.

Reading the Bible to See and Experience Jesus

Everyone wants to believe they are the main character in the story of their life. This isn't too surprising since we are naturally self-focused. It doesn't help that we are constantly being catered to in today's advertisement-obsessed culture. From car commercials to political campaigns, from billboards to clothing brands, almost everything we see further ingrains the idea that we are at the center of our own narratives.

The Bible isn't primarily a story about us but a wondrous epic about Jesus.

It is all too easy for us to read the Bible in the same way.

It's tempting to make Scripture all about us, obsessing over what each verse "means for me" instead of tuning in to the original purpose and meaning of the text. The Bible isn't primarily a story about us but a wondrous epic about Jesus. According to the Bible's grand story, Jesus is the central point of prophecy and human history. Everything before his birth, life, death, and resurrection points ahead to those events, and everything after his ascension refers back to him. In other words, in the Old Testament we look forward to his first coming, and in the New Testament we get to know his work and look forward to his return. There is room for only one main character, one protagonist, one hero, and that's Jesus, God's Son.

When we read the Bible, our goal is to look for Jesus in every page. We can see how the gospel fits into the words we're reading instead of placing it over the grid of our own agenda. Even better, we can also read Scripture prayerfully, experiencing the very presence of Jesus as we learn about and worship him.

Reading the Bible to Be Changed

When I was growing up in the Straw Bale House, the electricity often went out. It was especially frightening when we lost power at night and were surrounded by complete darkness. That's when my mom would grope through the dark, find her candle collection, and carefully light each wick. As the flames ignited, the darkness scattered, and all at once the power outage felt like an adventure rather than something to be scared of.

Scripture is like a candle in the darkness—or, more accurately, like the noonday sun. When the light of God's truth shines on us, it sends the darkness of our sin scattering.

When the words of God are paired with conviction from the Holy Spirit, they produce eternal change. When we read the Bible, God is reading us, and this power is what we walk into whenever we open God's Word.

We read the Bible with humility, knowing that the Word has authority over us, not the other way around. We don't bend Scripture to fit our agenda, our personality, or our tastes. Rather, we bring our brokenness before God's Word and ask the Holy Spirit to conform us to his design and purpose. It is good to come to the Bible hungry, lonely, and broken, because the truth of Scripture has the power to leave us satisfied, loved, and whole.

> *It is good to come to the Bible hungry, lonely, and broken, because the truth of Scripture has the power to leave us satisfied, loved, and whole.*

We can read the Bible with expectancy, even urgency, knowing that God is able to turn our brokenness into beauty and that he will use his revealed Word to do so.

Commentaries and Spiritual Literature

Bible reading is a nonnegotiable component of quiet time. If we don't fill our hearts and minds with the truth of Scripture, our time with the Lord will lack perspective, power, and peace. However, we don't need to *only* read the Bible!

Over the years, I've found that Christ-centered literature and commentaries are enjoyable and beneficial additions to my quiet time. While it's true that no book can compare to the Bible, it's also true that no Christian is an island. Many believers have gone before us in this journey of faith, and we can learn a great deal from their wisdom, insight, and study of Scripture.

Christ-Centered Literature

I started reading Christian books in earnest during my first year in the United States. Suddenly I had access to more books than I'd had in Mongolia, and once I realized the power of a library card, I started reading everything I could get my hands on. Eventually I started incorporating Christ-centered books into my quiet time. These books have helped to shape my thinking and broaden my perspective beyond my own little life. I've found that if I read a Christ-centered book just before reading the Bible, I am "warmed up," so to speak. This also gives the Word the final say before I go about my day.

But not all Christian books are created equal. It's important to be choosy about which books to read. A book can be called "Christian" simply because it's written by an author who claims to be a Christian or is marketed to a Christian audience. However, a Christian label doesn't give a book inherent merit. Some books in the Christian genre contain messages that range from misguided information to blatant false teaching.

As you decide what books to read, seek recommendations

from Christians whose judgment you trust. Do some digging to find out who endorses the book and what people have to say about it. As you read these books, use the Bible as a measuring stick for the content. While you won't agree with every word in everything you read, there are some books that are so contrary to the gospel that they're not worth your time. Instead, fill your life with content that will enrich your faith and draw you closer to the Lord.

A word of caution: while Christ-centered literature can enrich our quiet times, it's not a substitute for reading God's Word. It might be tempting to opt for a daily devotional instead of the Bible itself. This is understandable, since devotionals are easy to consume and often feature verses that are inoffensive and simple to understand. The problem is that devotionals are primarily focused on the thoughts of the author, which do not carry the same weight and authority as God's Word. Also, devotionals may not accurately reflect the context and meaning of the verses it's referencing. That's why devotionals and other Christ-centered books are better tasted as side dishes, while the Bible itself is to be devoured as our main meal.

Bible Commentaries

Bible commentaries are written to help readers understand Scripture more deeply. Typically the authors have invested hours into the study of particular books and passages, allowing us to benefit from their hard-earned insights. Commentaries can shed light on parts of Scripture that are difficult to understand, allowing us to see new connections, explore historical contexts, discover original definitions, and gather cultural background. While commentaries may be written at a more academic level than most Christian nonfiction, they are helpful in understanding specific books or texts in Scripture.

The easiest way to weave these studies into your Bible reading is to use a study Bible. Study Bibles provide notes and commentary in footnotes or margins, and you can refer to these as you make your way through a particular passage.

It's important to make sure the editor or author of the commentary you're reading is trustworthy. So once again, seek recommendations and do some research before diving into a commentary, and continually hold up their words against Scripture itself.

Filling Our Lives with Scripture

Although it's important to have a predetermined plan and routine for reading the Bible, our interaction with God's Word can and should extend beyond our daily quiet times. Scripture is meant to permeate every part of our lives, from our private devotions to our public interactions. If we are sufficiently shaped and influenced by God's Word, we'll be prepared to handle a variety of interactions, conversations, decisions, temptations, and difficult seasons. This important work of "renewing our minds" (Romans 12:2) ultimately involves a heart change, which comes from a growing understanding of Scripture and a deepening obedience to Jesus.

The following practices are just a few ways we can start

filling our minds and lives with more of God's Word. But first it's important to remember that these practices are *tools*, not *rules*. The grace of Jesus allows us to move at our own pace and capacity as we grow in these rhythms. I recommend that you start small—and don't feel like you need to do each of these every day! Remember: there are no deadlines or grading rubrics when it comes to spending time with Jesus!

Scripture Memorization

Scripture memorization involves selecting a specific verse or passage from Scripture and then committing it to memory. Our goal in memorizing is not perfection; rather, it's the effort itself that is worthwhile. As we memorize particular sections of Scripture, the words become at least somewhat ingrained into our subconscious. Then, even if we fail to remember the exact phrasing, we still find that certain passages and concepts spring to mind more readily, thanks to the Holy Spirit's prompting. If God's Word is at the top of our minds, we can better battle temptation, discern the truth, encourage suffering friends, and defend our faith.

There isn't one right way to memorize Scripture. You can study flash cards during a break at school or work, you can put Post-it Notes on your mirror or in your car, or you can use reminders on your phone. Other methods include writing the first letter of every word you're memorizing on your arm[4] or on a piece of paper so you can refer to it throughout the day. Another strategy is to choose a theme verse for every month of the year. No matter the details, committing Scripture to memory will always help us deepen and enjoy our walk with Jesus.

Scripture Meditation

Scripture meditation is dwelling on and savoring the words of Scripture and applying them to our lives. Like allowing a piece of chocolate to slowly melt in your mouth, meditation is letting a particular verse or passage sink into your soul.

While we don't need to be in a perfectly peaceful environment to meditate on Scripture, it does help to find a private, quiet place away from interruption. Of course, this isn't possible for everyone, especially in seasons when our lives overflow with hustle and bustle. If you're in a season of mothering young children, maintaining a sporadic college-class schedule, working overtime, or dealing with an illness, it will be harder to be still and think deeply about Scripture.

Denysha's Quiet-Time Story

As I read the Bible, I'm amazed at how relevant it is for whatever I'm going through. One passage that has been especially meaningful to me is Psalm 56:3: "When I am afraid, I will put my trust in you." I had a near-death experience several years ago, and as a result, I started struggling with anxiety. I held on to that verse when I was in the midst of that difficult season, and it continues to bring me hope and comfort now, with all the turmoil in our world.

No matter what season of life we're in, this isn't easy to do. Even when we find the time to be still, diversions are only a remote click or a phone scroll away. In our fast-paced, media-saturated world, meditating on God's Word has never been harder. But it's well worth the effort. When we quiet our hearts and minds to dwell on Scripture, we grow in self-control and gain tools we need to overcome our anxieties.

These moments of stillness likely won't just happen; they require intentionality, whether that means getting someone to watch your children while you take a walk or lying quietly in your dorm bed before your roommates return or even stepping into a bathroom stall for a few minutes during your lunch break. If you get creative, you can find miniretreats of silence, no matter how loud your surrounding world might be.

Some tools that can be helpful in Scripture meditation are flash cards, a Bible app on your phone, or a chalkboard in a prominent place in your home. You can use these tools to write down or bookmark a verse and then reread it throughout the day.

As we meditate on Scripture, we allow God's Word to travel from our heads into our hearts. In the process, the words become sweeter, dearer, and more beautiful to us than ever before.

Other Scripture Formats

There's more than one way to digest Scripture. Some people learn best by reading, while others benefit from listening to Scripture or viewing Bible-based videos (see the appendix on page 231 for suggestions). Never before has there been access to so much Scripture in so many different formats!

You don't always have to be sitting quietly with your Bible in your lap. You can listen to Scripture while you drive, you can meditate on a verse while doing dishes, or you can memorize a passage while folding laundry. Whatever method you choose, it's possible to saturate every part of your life with God's Word.

Be Uncommon

Let's face it: we live in a society that doesn't highly value the Word of God.

Our country is rife with cultural Christians—people who claim to follow Jesus but live in a way that contradicts what the Bible teaches. It's common enough for people to know a few verses offhand or remember the story of David and Goliath or own a throw pillow with Jeremiah 29:11 stitched on it. What's less common is to be someone who knows, loves, and obeys God's Word.

As of 2020, only 9 percent of American Christians said they read their Bible on a daily basis.[5] It isn't easy to give God's Word a place of such high priority in our lives . . . but we are called to be uncommon. We're called to be set apart in our allegiance to truth. God commands us to not conform to this world but to be transformed by the renewing of our minds (see Romans 12:1-2).

We can't coast when it comes to our commitment to Scripture. We must be ready to dig deeply into God's Word and make it the foundation of our lives. It's worth filling our lives with Scripture every day, because standing behind every word, there is a living, breathing God who delights in revealing himself to us.

your turn

Read

Joshua 1:8; Romans 12:2; 2 Timothy 3:16-17

Reflect

1. What has been your motivation for reading the Bible in the past? Which of the reasons listed in this chapter do you find most compelling?

2. As you approach reading Scripture, which of the "how to read the Bible" tips stand out to you, and why?

Grow

1. Select a Bible reading plan, and then either sign up for it or print it out. If you're not sure where to start, biblegateway .com has some good options.

2. Make a list of Christ-centered books and commentaries you might want to read. Then choose one to begin including as part of your daily quiet time.

3. Write down one verse you want to memorize and mediate on this month.

Pray

Dear Jesus, thank you for giving us your Word. Thank you for revealing your character through Scripture, and thank you for showing me who I am and how you want me to live in this world. Please help me to make reading the Bible a priority every day so I can fill my life with your truth. Help me to become uncommon in my love for your Word. Amen.

6

talking with Jesus

Becoming a Prayer Warrior

"I DON'T LOVE YOU."

My heart began to pound frantically and my vision blurred as my boyfriend of two years shared his true feelings. We were sitting in his living room—the same place we'd spoken about engagement rings not long before. I could hardly process the words he'd just uttered, a statement that was now burning a hole in my stomach.

I had met him during my second year in America. He was older, handsome, and ambitious, and he'd pursued me confidently. I was starstruck. His attention swept me away, and over the course of the next two years, I was convinced that this was the man God wanted me to marry. We went to church together, met for lunch every day, attended the same events, and even traveled on family vacations together. He had become the center of my world.

Now I was about to enter my senior year of college, and for the past several weeks we'd been going through premarital counseling with the expectation of engagement right around the corner. The last thing I expected to hear that night were the words *I don't love you*.

In a single moment, my world crumbled. My throat choked with tears as I tried to respond, but nothing seemed to come out right. I soon found myself running out of his house. I drove home through a rainstorm in the dark, sobbing uncontrollably.

What was supposed to be a season of joy and expectation turned into one of bitter disappointment. The grief of the breakup threw me into a state of melancholy that lasted for months. The nights were filled with agitated, restless sleep. The days were joyless and long, and life seemed to have lost its shine. I felt as though I would never be happy again.

But behind the scenes, God was at work, pulling my attention back to himself.

I was ashamed to admit it, but the past two years had slowly been leading me away from Jesus. The romance—and my obsession over it—had been subtly changing me into someone I was not. I had once been extroverted and silly, and now I was subdued and shy. I used to not care much about money or clothing, but now I was desperately trying to fit into the upper-class culture of my boyfriend's family.

Not only that, but my relationship with Jesus was slowly becoming less of a priority. My devotional routines suffered, my prayer time took a back seat, and my ambitions started to center around worldly definitions of success. I had even followed my boyfriend to a church that I knew was not teaching Scripture faithfully. At some level I knew the warning signs were there, but I chose to ignore or excuse them. I had placed romance and marriage on such a high pedestal that I was willing to sacrifice anything to have them.

However, God had a better plan than simply giving me what I wanted. Rather than let me self-destruct in the pursuit of my idols, the Lord was determined to restore me to himself.

I believe that the breakup was an act of God's severe mercy. It was an incredibly painful experience for me,

God has better plans than simply giving us what we want.

both thoroughly heartbreaking and utterly necessary. I had been gripping my desire for marriage so tightly that the Lord had to break my fingers to set me free. Yet as I worked my way through the grief of unexpected rejection, I started returning to a practice I had neglected for a long time: I began to pray again.

I prayed as I cried in the shower. I prayed as I ran around the block in an attempt to feel better. I prayed when I saw things that reminded me of my ex, and I prayed as I lay in bed overwhelmed by depression.

I cleaned out a spot in my closet and spent at least an hour there every day, pouring out my heart and my tears to my Savior. Soon my quiet time was once again the sweetest part of my day. Talking to Jesus provided a great relief from my pain, so I drank in his presence as if I were dying of thirst. It had been months since I'd conversed with God so consistently, and as my earthly romance faded into the past, my relationship with Jesus was being restored.

Fully Known and Fully Loved

While I was in this dating relationship, I felt like it was necessary to change who I was to become more lovable. Yet these efforts not only drove me to compromise my values but also caused me to lose the love I'd tried so hard to secure. After two years of swelling insecurity, it was a relief to be completely myself, to be vulnerable and genuine in the presence of someone who knew me perfectly yet truly loved me.

God alone is capable of fully knowing us *and* fully loving us, and that's what makes prayer such a sanctuary, especially for those with broken hearts. We might be able to conceal who we really are from other human beings, but it's impossible to fool God. With other people, we can assume a personality and pretend to be someone we're not. Even when such pretense fails, we can keep our deepest thoughts hidden from public view. However, none of this masquerading is possible with an all-knowing, all-seeing God.

Just as an artist knows every brushstroke on his canvas, so our Creator knows our every quirk, desire, weakness, fear, and freckle. He has counted the hairs on our heads and knitted each of us together in our mothers' wombs. He witnesses our every deed and knows our every thought. There is no attitude that God hasn't noticed, no secret sin he doesn't know about, and no failure that is hidden from his view.

Being fully known is a significant problem for sinners like us, because we naturally put conditions on our love for others based on how they behave, especially toward us. If we were capable of truly knowing each other—every thought, hidden motive, and flawed feature—we would struggle even more than we already do to love one other. Thankfully, God is not like us! His full knowledge of us drives him not away from us but *toward* us.

There has never been and there never will be anyone who loves us as deeply as God does. Even the love of a mother who is intoxicated with the beauty of her child can't compare with the love God has for the people made in his image. This is possible because God does not base his love for us on who we are or what we've done. Instead, God *is* love (see 1 John 4:8). He loves us simply because that's *who God is*.

However, God's love is not the same thing as his approval. Just like a parent who loves and longs for their wayward child, God can love us while also condemning our wrong behavior. Before I understood this, prayer was terribly difficult for me. I was so aware of my sin, and my guilt drove me away from prayer. I kept trying to be good so I could somehow earn the "right" to pray.

In the Old Testament, it was impossible for sinful people to stand before God without the buffer of a purifying ritual, an animal sacrifice, and a priestly order (see Exodus 40:1-15). Even then, only a few select people were allowed to enter the innermost sanctuary of God's holy presence. This place, called the Holy of Holies, was a place where no sin or blemish could survive, but it was also a place of amazing grace for those who were purified and approved to enter (see Hebrews 9:1-10).

The Old Testament sacrificial system wasn't God's final answer to our sin, however. It was only a foreshadowing of what was to come. At just the right moment in history, God showed his love by sending his Son, Jesus, to be the ultimate sacrifice for our sin. Now all those who believe in Jesus are not only fully known and fully loved but also fully accepted into the presence of God! Jesus is our door (see John 10:9) into the Holy of Holies, and now we can have unhindered access to the Father in prayer (see Hebrews 9:11-28).

These truths have helped me realize the true splendor and pleasure of prayer. If God fully knows me, then there's no one I can be more vulnerable and honest with. If God fully loves me, then there's no one I can trust more with my deepest longings and desires. And if I'm fully purified and approved in Christ, then I can converse with God any time, no matter what I've done. My sin is no longer a reason to avoid my Maker.

Why We Pray

During those long months of healing from my breakup, I was desperate for the balm of true love. I didn't need another flawed person to try to fill in the cracks of my heart. I needed communion with the God who created me, knows me, and loves me. This is why prayer became the highlight of my days during that season. Prayer is a response to the love God has shown us. Because of Jesus, we can approach him freely and pray without fear.

Regular prayer is one of the most valuable habits a Christian can establish. While there are many reasons to pray, there are three I find myself returning to again and again.

We Pray to Worship and Give Thanks

Love is something that cannot be kept quiet.

As a man and woman stand at the altar and express their commitment to and adoration for each other, their marriage becomes official and their love is confirmed. While it's true

Braulia's Quiet-Time Story

Quiet time is important to me because it's where I find joy, peace, and strength for the day and where I am filled with God's love. When I'm filled up myself, I can extend that love and mercy to my family and others. It's God's Word and my time in prayer that transform me into the likeness of Christ. The Lord was intentional about spending time in prayer, and we are called to follow his example. Apart from God, we can do nothing, so spending time in his presence is our lifeline—the best investment we can make. It's where we can find the rest, hope, joy, strength, encouragement, comfort, love, mercy, and wisdom that our souls deeply need.

that actions may speak louder than words, words are also necessary, especially when it comes to communicating love.

This is also true in our relationship with God.

If we claim to love the Lord but never take the time to tell him that, it's likely a sign that something is off. When we don't express adoration directly to the object of our love, our relationship becomes a performance for others rather than a genuine delight.

Prayer is putting words to our worship and giving them as an offering of love directly to God. I've found that as I intentionally express words of worship, my enjoyment of the Lord deepens. In turn, this leads into even more worship. Prayers of adoration put our focus on who God is—his beauty, character, and worthiness.

Just as prayers of adoration pull our attention back to who God is, prayers of gratitude remind us of what God has done for us. Voicing our gratitude to him keeps our hearts in a posture of worship. From the breaths we take to the people in our lives, God has given us innumerable and lavish gifts. These blessings are best enjoyed when the Giver is appreciated. In other words, our love will increase the more we express it!

We Pray to Confess and Be Free

I have always been afraid of the dark.

Ever since I was little, I've experienced a small spike of fear whenever the lights go out. Suddenly my familiar world is cast into shadow, and my imagination starts to run wild. Creatures start crawling along the ceiling, faces materialize out of dark corners, and normal nighttime noises become a cacophony of ill-intentioned guests. As a child, all I could do to shut out my fear was pull the covers over my head until I fell asleep.

Most of the time, my fear of the dark is unjustified. But after living in the subtropics of Florida for more than a decade, I've come to learn that a shadow moving in the night might actually be more than my imagination. Large— I mean *really* large—wolf spiders and cockroaches are notorious for finding their way inside, and I've had more than one experience with these intruders. When this happens, it's not enough to pull the covers over my head like I did as a child. If there's a real critter on the floor, wall, ceiling, or even on my bedspread (yes, that has happened!), the only way to deal with it is to turn on the light and reveal the shadow for what it is. Once the truth is revealed, I can do what it takes to dispatch the trespasser and get back to sleep.

This is true for our sin as well.

Just as darkness gives power to fear and creates monsters out of empty spaces, sin finds its power in darkness. It wants nothing more than to remain in shadow and hold us hostage under a blanket of denial and ignorance. However, as soon as we shine the light of confession on our sin, the power of sin is broken. As we walk in confession, repentance, and freedom, sin stops looking so daunting.

This is another reason we pray: to confess our sin and ask the Lord to help us change so we can be set free by the power of the Holy Spirit.

We Pray to Intercede and Receive

"All we can do is pray."

This is something I used to say when I felt like I'd reached the limit of my capacity to help someone. But as I learned more about the power of prayer, my heart was convicted. Prayer is not a last resort; it's a first course of action! In reality, our prayers are the best thing we can give someone else, because in prayer we have access to the riches of God's help and provision. The best way to love someone is by praying for them.

Prayer is not a last resort; it's a first course of action!

While there is only so much time, money, and energy we can give other people, God's resources, abilities, gifts, and love are limitless. So whether a friend is struggling with sin, experiencing a physical need, or walking through suffering, our first step should be to pray. No one can provide for them like God can. He alone is all powerful, and only he knows what's best for each of us. When we intercede for others, we hand over to God the work that we can't do ourselves. We are trusting him to act in whatever way he knows is best. And as we pray, God will often convict us to action and show us practical ways to love others.

This kind of prayer applies to our own needs as well.

When we're faced with an over-whelming situation or need, or with what may seem like a trivial challenge or desire, we can turn to God for wisdom and provision. God cares about every aspect of our lives, big

When we intercede for others, we hand over to God the work that we can't do ourselves.

and small, and he has promised to provide according to his good purposes for us. Knowing we have a Father who desires our ultimate good, we can boldly ask him for anything and everything, trusting that whether he says yes or no, he does so from a place of love.

As we come to him expectantly and experience his answers to our prayers, our faith will continually be strengthened.

How We Pray

My guess is that we all *want* to pray and we know we *should* pray. But how do we actually go about doing it? There is no magic formula for praying, and there are no perfect words God expects us to say. But there are a few heart postures we can pay attention to so we can pray more effectively. When Jesus prayed, he modeled humility, expectancy, and honesty, and we can follow his example (see John 17).

We Pray Humbly

It's easy to go into prayer with a demanding spirit. We are naturally prideful, so we tend to assume we know exactly what we need or what should happen in any given situation.

It's good to share what's on our hearts with the Lord, but we also need to temper our desires with the words "not my will, but yours be done" (Luke 22:42). When we pray with humility, we are trusting God to do what's best instead of telling him what to do.

God loves us too much to give in to our every demand, no matter how much sense our request makes to us. Humble prayers help us remain thankful and even joyful when God's answer is different from what we hoped for.

We Pray Expectantly

Because of Christ, we can come before the throne of grace boldly and expectantly. Romans 8:26-27 says that the Holy Spirit intercedes on our behalf before the Father, especially when we don't know how to pray. This gives us the confidence to pray with hopeful expectation.

Another reason we can pray expectantly is because God is all powerful. He can move heaven and earth to work on our behalf or on behalf of someone we're interceding for. This truth has grown in me an eagerness to pray about everything, from small requests to seemingly impossible dreams. There's nothing too large for God to handle and nothing too small for him not to care about. Everything—absolutely everything—is okay to talk with God about. From our desire to get over a cold to our need for financial provision to our desperate longing to see someone come to faith in Christ, we can pray about all of it. After all, God owns everything (see 1 Corinthians 10:26), and he withholds no good thing from those who love and walk with him (see Psalm 84:11 and Romans 8:28).

If we don't pray with expectation, we run the risk of missing out on extraordinary answers to prayer. James, the half-brother of Jesus, said this about prayer: "You do not have because you do not ask God" (James 4:2). That means we should ask, ask, ask! However, our boldness must be guided by the truth of God's Word. In the next sentence James says, "When you ask, you do not receive, because you ask with wrong motives, that you may spend what you get on your pleasures" (James 4:3). God is not a vending machine that gives us what we want if we just insert enough faith. Rather, he is an eternally wise, completely sovereign, and all-powerful being who wants us to trust his decisions. No matter how God responds to our prayers, we can have faith that he will do what's best for his glory and our eternal good.

We Pray Honestly

God knows us fully and loves us fully, so we can pray with complete honesty and transparency. There's no need for pretense when approaching the Father, no need for fancy language, no need to sweep our true emotions under the rug. As human beings who were made to experience all kinds of feelings, we can take those emotions directly to the Creator and submit them to him without fear of rejection.

There is no better example of honest prayers than the book

of Psalms. The words throughout these pages express a wide range of emotions, from white-hot anger to soul-drowning sorrow, from out-of-this-world joy to lonely despair. As we read the Psalms, we see what it looks like to be transparent toward God, no matter how messy it looks. We learn that conversing with the Lord gives us an opportunity to expose and express the deepest places of our hearts.

The Lord desires to walk with us through every season, and one of the ways we can welcome him into every part of our lives is by praying honestly. He is a loving Father, and he wants our relationship with him to be built on genuine trust and closeness. So we can pray honestly in his presence, expressing everything we think and feel. God can handle all of it. As long as we pair our honesty with submission to his will, there is never such a thing as getting "too emotional" in prayer.

Becoming a Prayer Warrior

All around us there is a battle raging—in the lives of our Christian brothers and sisters, in the lives of those who don't know Christ, and in our own lives. This battle is a spiritual one, and prayer is one of the most strategic ways for us to take up arms and join the fight. As soon as we begin to pray, we step onto the battlefield, where we fight side by side with an all-powerful King to defeat the spiritual forces of darkness. Prayer is indispensable for defeating sin, engaging in meaningful work, and bringing souls into the Kingdom of Jesus.

There is nothing more threatening to the devil than a Christian who prays.

In order to fulfill our calling as prayer warriors, we need to be intentional about praying on a regular basis. We can't expect prayer to spontaneously happen just because we claim to know Christ. As with Bible reading, prayer needs to begin as an intentional habit before it becomes second nature.

When it comes to prayer, there are two main habits we need to cultivate: praying alone and praying with other people.

Praying Alone

We see the value of private prayer portrayed in the life of Jesus. If the Son of God made it a point to escape the crowds and get alone with the Father, then so should we. This is how we tend to our personal relationship with him and how we are strengthened for battle.

Heidi's Quiet-Time Story

Strangely enough, the season when I've felt closest to God is when I was literally out of money. I sent out more than sixty résumés over the course of two and a half months, and I didn't get a single offer. I prayed so much and spent so much time in the Word in that season. As difficult as that time was, I wouldn't trade it. I've never felt so close to God, because he was all I had.

To make private prayer happen, we need to choose a time and a place, and then we simply need to show up. I've found that private prayer works best when it's included in a daily quiet-time routine. As with Bible reading, our prayer goals should start small and grow from there. We don't want to get overwhelmed by an expectation to pray for an hour every day or go through a lengthy list of requests. This is a recipe for burnout. Instead, it's wise to evaluate our life circumstances to determine how long of a prayer time makes sense for this season. You may be able to pray for long periods of time and really sink into the experience right now, or you may be in a season when it's difficult to squeeze in five minutes of private, uninterrupted prayer. While the length of time may look different for everyone, we all need alone time with God, no matter how long that time may be.

As part of your prayer time, you might want to keep a prayer list. Lists can help us stay focused and help us remember what we want to pray about. Another helpful tool is a prayer outline, which keeps us aligned with an attitude of humility, expectancy, and honesty.

Jesus himself gave us an outline when he taught his disciples the Lord's Prayer in Matthew 6:9-13:

Our Father in heaven,
hallowed be your name,
your kingdom come,
your will be done,

on earth as it is in heaven.
Give us today our daily bread.
And forgive us our debts,
    as we also have forgiven
        our debtors.
And lead us not into temptation,
    but deliver us from the evil one.

In the mid-1990s, the late author Elisabeth Elliot came to speak at a conference for women missionaries in Mongolia. As one of the event organizers, my mom got to meet and speak with Elisabeth. Over the course of one of their conversations, Elisabeth told my mom she believed that the Lord's Prayer contains everything we need to pray about on a daily basis. This conversation has stuck with my mom through the years, and she passed on these words of wisdom to me. If we use the Lord's Prayer as a thematic outline for our conversations with God, we will cover every topic we need to pray about.

Another meaningful way to converse with Christ is to pray through Scripture. Doing this can help us apply what we're reading in the Bible to our own lives and the lives of those around us. Using Scripture can guide our conversations and expand the content of our prayers.

God does not require us to take certain physical postures when we pray, but there are benefits to doing so, because what we do physically can affect our attitudes. For example, closing our eyes, praying out loud, lifting our hands, or getting down on our knees can help direct our focus heavenward and keep us in a place of humility and worship.

Praying Together

The other way we converse with Jesus is by gathering and praying with other believers. This practice may be overlooked in conversations about quiet time, since daily devotions are often viewed as a solo practice. However, as Christians, we have been adopted into a family, which means talking to our Father is also a communal activity.

Eternity is moved when Christians pray together. There is power when we come before God in unity with our spiritual brothers and sisters and make our requests known to him. One of the best ways to incorporate communal prayer into your spiritual habits is by reaching out to your closest Christian friends and committing to praying together. Even if just two or three of you gather, the Lord will be with you and hear your prayers (see Matthew 18:20). Eventually your group may grow, and extraordinary things will certainly result! Love will blossom, sin will be defeated, and lives will be changed when we pray together (see 1 John 5:14-15).

The good news is that our prayers don't have to be isolated to small groups and prayer closets! With practice, prayer can become a natural part of our relationships. When a need arises, we pause and pray immediately. When someone expresses a burden, we pray for them right then and there. When our families bring up a difficult topic around the dinner table, we take a moment to pray. When we go on coffee dates or have phone calls with friends, we pray before parting. Over time, prayer can become part of our ordinary, everyday interactions.

He Gives Us Rest

As we each seek to grow in our prayer habits, God promises an abundance of grace. Even as we learn to be more intentional about praying in private and with others, we can rest easy, knowing it's not about performing but about being with Jesus and talking with him about anything and everything.

Prayer isn't about kneeling a certain number of times a day, chanting particular words over and over, or going through the motions of a religious ceremony. Prayer is about laying bare the deepest places of our hearts and allowing God to enter and do his will. Prayer is less about striving and more about surrender.

Prayer is less about striving and more about surrender.

In prayer we can quiet our hearts, focus on who God is and what he has done, and give ourselves over to the joy of having direct access to the one who loves us. In prayer we can make our longings known and trust that he will do what is best.

your turn

Read

Matthew 6:5-13

Reflect

1. What are your reasons for wanting to pray? What are some of the reasons you struggle to pray?

2. Which posture of prayer do you want to focus on this week: humility, expectancy, or honesty?

Grow

1. Create three prayer lists:

   - a list of things you're grateful for
   - a list of requests on behalf of others
   - a list of personal requests

   Commit to praying about at least one item from each list during your quiet time.

2. Identify two or three friends you'd like to pray with, and set up a time to meet to pray together.

Pray

Dear Jesus, thank you for making it possible for me to pray to you. Thank you for knowing and loving me fully. Help me not to take the privilege of speaking with you for granted. Strengthen my faith in your ability to answer my prayers, and help me to trust that no matter what answer you give, you will do what's best for me and those around me. By your grace and through the power of your Holy Spirit, make me a prayer warrior on behalf of your Kingdom. Amen.

getting creative

Quiet-Time Ruts and How to Get Out of Them

IT WAS THE SUMMER OF 2015.

I had just graduated college, and the burdens of school along with the painful breakup from the year before were starting to fade. After graduating with a degree in graphic design, I bought a camera and launched a wedding photography business. I spent my days taking and editing pictures, assisting a local wedding-planning company, and taking on freelance graphic design work to make ends meet. The transition from college to career, though intense, was more fun than I'd expected it to be.

Life was filled with exciting possibilities. I enjoyed the challenges of owning my own small business, and it was exhilarating to see my calendar fill up with clients from all over the country. However, along with the change of season came a spiritual struggle—one I'd experienced before but wasn't quite sure what to call.

I was becoming bored in my relationship with the Lord.

The fuller my calendar became, the more complacent my heart grew toward God. This attitude manifested itself in my daily quiet time, which seemed drained of all enjoyment. Although I was still reading the Bible and praying consistently, my heart didn't seem to be as engaged as it once was. Life was exciting, but my time with the Lord wasn't. Eventually, I came up with a name for my predicament, which I called a "quiet-time rut."

Thankfully, by that time I'd learned that challenging quiet-time seasons are not a reflection of my position in Christ; rather, they're emotional turns that show up in the life of every believer. I knew if I just kept pushing through, this season would pass. However, I also didn't want to sit back and do nothing! So I began exploring ways to infuse joy and interest back into my time with the Lord.

It was time to shake things up.

Quiet-Time Ruts

All of us experience emotional ruts at some point in our walk with Jesus. It's an unavoidable part of being human, but thankfully God knows and understands. Unlike the long slog of quiet-time drudgery (see chapter 3), quiet-time ruts pop up briefly throughout our lives and usually have an underlying cause that we can address relatively quickly. Some quiet-time ruts can often be resolved within a day or two of moving some things around, whereas drudgery can take months or even years to give way to discipline and delight. That said, it's important to try to decipher where the emotional clog is coming from so we can work to resolve it. A time of lethargy can be caused by a number of factors, such as unrelenting distractions, unrepentant sin, or ongoing suffering. But with the help of the Holy Spirit, we can come up with creative ways to break free.

The Rut of Distraction

A common ditch we may fall into is the rut of distraction.

The cares of this world along with an overly packed schedule are enough to drain any heart of peace and joy. As a result, we have quiet times

Sofia's Quiet-Time Story

One of my favorite things about spending quiet time with Jesus is being able to look back in my journal and see how far I've come in my relationship with him and in learning his Word. Through all the ups and downs of my life, Jesus has been the constant who has brought peace, guidance, grace, and strength. Finding a moment to spend time with our Maker makes us more aware of our dependence on him—creating humble, thankful hearts in us every day.

that lack focus, we miss opportunities to love and care for others, and we forget to spend time with the Lord altogether because we're too busy doing other things.

The rut of distraction is a sneaky one, mainly because the distractions that fill our lives are often good things. A career, work around the home, relationships, trip planning, the endless cycle of social media—these are just a few of the distractions that can pull us away from time with the Lord.

This is the rut I most commonly find myself in.

I'm someone who thrives with a full schedule and packed to-do list. This isn't a bad thing in itself, but I can easily become overloaded with self-imposed expectations. As a result, my quiet time suffers, my peace is threatened, and my enjoyment in Jesus is diminished.

Realistically, no life can be totally free from distractions. Unless we withdraw from the world altogether, there will always be people who need us and jobs that need to be done. However, it is possible to create healthy margins to manage the demands on our attention. Margins allow us to slow down, breathe deeply, and focus on the present. They give us the space to accomplish each task peacefully instead of always rushing to the next activity or appointment.

When we find ourselves continually distracted from our relationship with Jesus, it's time to start evaluating and cutting commitments from our schedules. Purposefully saying no is a way to protect our hearts from drifting and protect our enjoyment of the Lord.

The Rut of Sin

Sometimes we experience emotional distance from the Lord because of unrepentant sin. Although we've been justified in Christ and are sanctified through the power of the Holy Spirit, sin still has a way of weaseling into our lives. It can wreak destruction if we're not vigilant about guarding against it.

Just as a husband and wife need to work through an argument and forgive one another before they can sleep peacefully in each other's arms, so we need to confess and repent of our sin before we can savor the Lord's presence. This doesn't mean we need to be perfect before coming to our quiet time; it just means it's impossible to hide, justify, or wallow in our sin. To cling to our sin is to shut Christ out, and if we do, our intimacy with him will suffer.

While all unconfessed sin plagues us, sin against another person can especially separate us from enjoying God's presence. God loves the one we sinned against just as much as he loves us, and he won't let our hearts be at peace until we go to our brother or sister and ask for forgiveness (see Matthew 5:24).

Sin must be taken seriously. During our quiet time, we have the opportunity to lay our struggles at the altar and choose a relationship with Christ over our selfish desires.

The Rut of Suffering

Another common quiet-time rut is brought about by suffering. Our emotions are deeply affected by hard times, whether the suffering is physical, mental, or relational. And because our relationship with God is intrinsically connected to every other part of our being, suffering can put a damper on our quiet times.

Sometimes the opposite is true as well. By his grace, God can use suffering to draw us into his presence like never before. While the world suffers without hope, we can rejoice with the promise of eternity, even as our hearts and bodies ache. This doesn't mean we will necessarily feel grace-filled in the moment. Seasons of grief can take hold of us, body, mind, and soul, and sometimes the most we can do is simply cling to the Cross and pray for the dawn. Joy may come in the morning, but the dark night of suffering certainly can be long (see Psalm 30:5).

If you are experiencing a quiet-time rut brought about by suffering, the best medicines are time, the truth of God's Word, and the comfort of God's people. When enduring suffering, we may need to remain loyal to our current quiet-time structure in order to maintain consistency, or we may benefit from shifting our quiet-time expectations for a season. In either case, it's vital for us to cling to the Cross of Jesus in our grief. Just as Peter walked on the waves toward Jesus, we must keep our eyes fixed on the Savior in order to stay above the swelling tides of tragedy, illness, loss, and relational heartbreak.

We will inevitably fall into quiet-time ruts at some point, and when we do, we should feel free to get creative in our relationship with the Lord. Sometimes shaking things up or introducing a new quiet-time element will help restore our joy in spending time with Jesus.

I've found that one of the best ways to ward off emotional ruts in my quiet time is by keeping a journal.

Putting Pen to Paper

I started my first journal when I was eight years old.

Ever since, I've kept a detailed account of the events in my life, as well as the inner workings of my heart. I've recorded my thoughts in a variety of books—from hardbound to paperback, from faux leather to sparkly. My life's journey unfolds across pages of hesitant scribbles and passionate strokes, revealing a tapestry of God's loving faithfulness.

Every once in a while, I open the cedar chest that contains these precious journals and let myself get lost in the years gone by. Every time I read through the well-worn pages, I'm reminded of how God has guided and directed my every step. This habit of recording my thoughts has become one of the most enjoyable elements of my daily quiet time.

While journaling is a good fit for me, I recognize that it's not for everyone. Reading the Bible and praying are the only two nonnegotiables of a daily quiet time—anything else is a bonus! However, journaling can bring richness and enjoyment into our daily time with Jesus.

Here are just a few of the reasons you might consider

starting a journal, especially if you find yourself stuck in a quiet-time rut.

Journaling Helps Us Process Our Emotions

One of the greatest benefits of journaling is that it gives us the ability to express and process our emotions. The act of writing something down requires us to formulate our thoughts, and as we think through our feelings and pin them down, our understanding of them gets clearer.

I learned this during the season right after college. The day after my breakup, I got a brand-new journal and designated it for the purpose of expressing my disappointment and anger. The pages quickly filled with Psalms-inspired laments, messy venting sessions, and unpolished prayers that attempted to put my sadness into words. The process was cathartic. Journaling kept me from bottling up my emotions and allowed me to begin climbing out of my heartache.

Being able to take our thoughts out of the seclusion of our minds and place them in the light of bright white pages can release us from the power of lies, confusion, and doubt.

Journaling Preserves Our Memories

One of my all-time favorite activities is watching old home videos. We only have two tapes from our home-video collection that still run, but they are unparalleled treasures in my eyes. Within these recordings are sights and sounds from eras past, from a time when I spoke with a lisp and my parents looked like a couple of kids. Whether I'm watching home videos, looking through old photo albums, or perusing disheveled scrapbooks, I can't help but smile when I relive memories of where I came from and who I used to be.

Our lives are full of stories that we can learn from, laugh over, and pass down to our children. However, unless we take the time to record these stories, they will likely be lost. Memories must be captured or recorded in some way, whether by picture, video, or pen, in order to ensure that they continue to be treasured as the years go by.

Journaling is one of the easiest ways to keep our memories safe. Whenever I look through my old journals, I'm reminded of events I never would have remembered if I hadn't written them down. There are stories that make me laugh, cry, and sigh. There are stories that reveal the richness of life and

Jasmine's Quiet-Time Story

I'm currently in a season of singleness and just trying to figure out the next stage of my life while so much around me is changing. Between work, studies, and writing my dissertation, it's sometimes difficult to carve out time with the Lord. One thing that helps me with my quiet time is to do it in different places around the house—in my bedroom, in the sunroom, or in the yard. Sometimes I even do it in the car in between other activities. I love incorporating worship music into my time with the Lord, either starting or ending that way. I also like to have gel highlighters, sticky notes, faith stickers, and my trusty gold pen at hand to help me capture what I'm learning.

the love God has blessed me with over the years. And who knows—they may even give future generations the opportunity to learn from my own experiences.

Journaling Reminds Us of God's Provision

The main reason I journal is to remind myself of God's faithfulness and provision.

Sometimes when I'm feeling anxious about something, I try to remember something I was afraid of or anxious about in the past. It usually doesn't take long for me to find a journal entry that expresses a worry or a burden that was once on my mind. When I reread the details of my old fear, I realize that all the anxiety that had plagued me back then is completely gone! God has been faithful to provide for me in every difficulty, and my old journals remind me of that fact.

I can't even count the number of times I've pleaded with the Lord from the depths of my anxiety, only to forget all about my anguish as soon as my prayers were answered. We tend to have short memories when it comes to God's provision, which is why it's important to be intentional about remembering. We need to remember the answers God gives us, the times he has been faithful to us, and the ways he has provided for us.

Journaling helps us remember God's past provision and builds our present and future trust in him. When we record the ways God has answered our prayers and has come through for us in the challenges we face, we are encouraged to trust him when we face new difficulties.

Making a Joyful Noise

Music has always been a key part of my life. Whether it was my mom leading us in hymns before our homeschool day started or my dad strumming the "Belly Button" song on his guitar as we danced around the living room or my years of plunking out tunes on the piano, music has always spoken to my heart in ways nothing else can.

When I was a teenager, my mom gave me a *Celebration Hymnal*, and it didn't take long for the pages to become dog-eared and covered with rainbow sticker tabs. That hymnal traveled with me across the ocean when I moved to the States, and it continues to sit on the bookshelf next to my Bible. Whenever I need to coax my heart out of numbness and into delight, I take the hymnal down from the shelf and spend a few minutes singing through the old, familiar songs.

Music is powerful. It has a way of moving us and engaging the deepest parts of our hearts. The right combination of notes can strike a chord in us, pulling us out of ourselves and lifting our souls heavenward.

One of the best ways to become emotionally reengaged with the Lord is to bring music into our routine. Whether we're singing hymns a capella, pressing play on a worship song, or pulling out an old guitar, we can utilize God's gift of music to draw our gaze back to him. Music was created by God himself, and it can fill our hearts with great joy. At its best, music can serve as a gateway to worship, with the power to break down our pride, open our eyes, and rekindle our passion for Christ.

Music Expresses and Influences Our Emotions

Music has a way of both expressing and shaping our emotions. Songs of praise can shift our hearts away from an attitude of complaint and toward a spirit of contentment. Songs of lament can help us express deep grief. Some musical genres are used to vent anger (just ask my husband, who was a metal vocalist in a touring band for several years!), and others are lullabies meant to put the listener to sleep. Music has the power to give voice to what we feel—and the power to change us.

> *Music has a way of breaking through our hardness of heart and moving us toward deeper intimacy with God.*

I often sing when I'm going about my day, and I've started to notice there's a pattern to when and why I sing. I sing when I'm sad in order to feel better. I sing when I'm stressed to settle my mind. I sing when I'm happy because I just can't keep my good mood quiet! At times I feel something so deeply that words just aren't adequate. Every once in a while, I even sing my own song, letting the lyrics and the melody flow out of me unplanned and unhindered. These are the moments when any dignified pretense falls away, and I am able to worship genuinely, without the need to impress anyone.

If we want to guide our feelings back to God, bringing

song into our quiet times is a good way to do it. Music can help us break through hardness of heart, express our struggles or joys, and move us toward a deeper intimacy with God.

Music Helps Us Retain Truth

There's a reason we were taught the alphabet song in school. Putting a long string of facts (or letters!) to a melody makes us more likely to recall them later. Why? Because we generally remember feelings more easily than facts, and music directly engages our emotions. Whenever we hear a melody we've heard before, our brains subtly remind us of the way we felt when we first heard it, along with the lyrics that came with the melody. That's why Christmas music can be so nostalgic! Every time we hear a familiar melody, the feelings return and the lyrics become more solidified in our memory.

Whether we realize it or not, the lyrics to the songs we hear become ingrained in our memories, and over time they have the power to influence our outlook and beliefs. That doesn't mean we should never listen to secular music, but it does mean we should be intentional about the messages we plant in our hearts. And when it comes to worship, it's essential to choose songs that contain God-honoring, scripturally sound truth. With so many theologically rich worship songs available, there's no reason to settle for anything less!

When we learn hymns, sing psalms, and listen to Christ-centered songs, it helps us break out of the quiet-time doldrums and fill our hearts with truth. I may never have large swaths of Scripture perfectly memorized, but I'll always carry with me the theologically rich hymns of my youth. These lyrics come to the forefront whenever the familiar melodies begin to play. Lord willing, I hope to pass on these hymns to the next generation too.

Music Reminds Us That We're Not Alone

One of my favorite hymn writers is Fanny Crosby, who was born in 1820. Over the course of her ninety-five years, she wrote more than nine thousand hymns and gospel songs, including "Blessed Assurance" and "Pass Me Not, O Gentle Savior." What makes her story even more notable is that Fanny became blind at just six weeks old. With no memory of being able to see, Fanny joyfully exulted, "When I get to heaven, the first face that shall ever gladden my sight will be that of my Savior."[6]

Hymns and worship songs remind us that we're not alone. Every Christ-centered song we sing has a story and a person behind it—someone who gave their life to Christ and then walked through the hills and valleys in this journey of faith. While it's easy to feel like we're the only ones to struggle with particular challenges or sufferings, hymns remind us that we're not alone in walking this pilgrim's road. Lyrics penned by other believers can provide great comfort to us, reminding us that we're surrounded by a beautiful cloud of witnesses (see Hebrews 12:1).

Incorporating music to our quiet time is almost guaranteed to spark joy and new life to our hearts.

Changing Your Scenery

Sometimes breaking out of a quiet-time rut is as simple as walking outside. Habits can occasionally become a little too predictable, and we forget just how amazing it is to spend time in the presence of a holy God. When this happens, it's helpful to switch up our quiet-time location or even reorganize the space around us.

Here are three ways to change the scenery and, in doing so, breathe new life into your quiet time.

Go on a Walk

I'm the kind of person who would forget to go outside if I didn't have to. You can often find me bent over a computer screen, curled up on the couch with a book, or standing in front of my sink doing dishes. Although I love the sunlight that comes through my windows, I regularly forget just how much I need to go outside and stand under the big blue sky! When I finally make it outside, I'm almost instantly refreshed. The sun on my face reminds me of the Creator's glory, and the breeze in my hair draws me back to his love.

For most of us, the majority of our days take place inside. With the potential to work from home and even have groceries delivered right to our doorsteps, we may find ourselves moving from room to room without ever

There's a world full of natural wonders that can lift our spirits and woo our hearts to a deeper love for our Maker.

stepping foot out the front door. While we can be thankful for shelter and warmth, we shouldn't forget that there's a world full of natural wonders that can lift our spirits and woo our hearts to a deeper love for our Maker.

Of course, not everyone has access to a beautiful place to walk or a safe place to sit outside. But it's well worth the effort to find some way to get fresh air. Sitting on a front porch or taking a walk during your time with Jesus can help us renew our enjoyment of him.

Choose a New Quiet-Time Spot

I have a designated spot for my quiet time every day. Knowing where to go for prayer and Bible reading makes it easier to keep up the routine. (I happen to love the far-left corner of my comfy couch.) While sitting in the same spot every day to spend time with Jesus can be helpful in habit building, sometimes we need to shake things up— especially if we find ourselves struggling with boredom or complacency.

In some cases, refreshing our quiet time can be as simple as sitting in a different chair or going to the dining room table, where we can lay all our books in front of us. The act of getting up and having a new vantage point can breathe fresh life into our spiritual disciplines.

Another option for changing the scenery is to move the

furniture around. I love turning a blank room into a cozy spot, complete with warm lighting, throw blankets, and shelves filled with sentimental details. I've found that reorganizing the space I'm in gives me energy and makes me feel more peaceful when I pray.

It may not sound especially spiritual, but God created us with the capacity to turn our living space into a home. Whether it's a studio apartment, a dorm room, or a single-family home, we will enjoy our routines more when they can be done in a beautiful space. While it isn't necessary to do a full home makeover to climb out of a quiet-time rut, just reorganizing your bedroom or shifting a piece of furniture can breathe new life into your everyday routines.

Declutter Your Quiet-Time Spot

Of course, communing with Christ can happen anywhere, no matter how messy or distracting our surroundings may be. Yet when we can create a space free of chaos, it reduces mental and visual distractions. Even if you don't have the time or energy to clean the whole house, it helps to clear out a clutter-free space where you can focus on Jesus. In my own life, I've found that external order can often pave the way for internal peace.

He Gives Us Grace

As emotional beings who go through a variety of ups and downs, we shouldn't be surprised when our feelings don't line up with our faith. At some point, every routine will be derailed by distraction or get blocked by sin or fall headlong into the valley of suffering. When those seasons arrive, it helps to have a game plan.

Sometimes the solution is as easy as opening a hymnal or moving our furniture around. Other times, no matter how hard we try to break free, our spiritual routines remain firmly stuck in the rut of our circumstances. This is when we cast ourselves wholly upon the grace of God, trusting him to redeem our quiet time and bring us back to a place of authenticity and enjoyment.

Spending time with Jesus was never meant to be a fixed checklist or an unchangeable assignment.

Spending time with Jesus was never meant to be a fixed checklist or an unchangeable assignment. Our habits and daily rhythms are tweakable. When we allow the Holy Spirit to guide our habits, we experience the freedom and flexibility that come with being in a relationship with a God who loves us.

your turn

Read

Psalm 145

Reflect

1. Are you in a quiet-time rut right now?

2. If you are in a rut, do you think it's caused by distraction, sin, or suffering?

Grow

1. If you're in a rut of distraction, write down the things that are distracting you, as well as one or two ideas for eliminating unnecessary distractions.

2. If you're in a rut of sin, identify what's driving you away from Jesus. Confess this sin to the Lord, and then confess it to another Christian.

3. If you're in a rut of suffering, journal about the pain you're currently experiencing. Reach out to a close Christian friend and ask them to pray for you. Choose a verse from the Psalms as your theme for this season.

Pray

Dear Jesus, thank you that your love for me never changes, even when I fall into seasons of distraction, sin, or suffering. Please help me not to grow stagnant in my quiet time, and help me to always be looking for ways to deepen the time I spend in your presence. Show me if I'm currently in a quiet-time rut, and pull me out by the power of your Spirit. Breathe new joy and life into my relationship with you. Amen.

letting the Lord lead

The Holy Spirit's Role in Our Quiet Time

IT WAS A MONDAY NIGHT IN EARLY MARCH, and I was feeling nervous.

I was preparing to attend a Bible study for young professionals at a nearby church, and I just *knew* my ex-boyfriend was going to be there. Even though our breakup was several months earlier, I still dreaded our chance encounters around town. Seeing him was uncomfortable at best and, more often, completely unnerving. But I was determined not to let the awkwardness keep me from meeting new people and enjoying Christian fellowship. So when the time came, I took a deep breath, got in my car, and drove to the church.

I arrived to find a group of young adults playing cornhole

in one of the church courtyards. Sure enough, I glimpsed my ex meandering through the gathering. For a split second, I considered turning around and going home. However, I forced myself to walk toward the group, all the while bracing myself for what was sure to be a difficult evening. When I stepped into the courtyard, I fully expected to meet the blue-eyed stare of the man who had dumped me. To my surprise, I found myself looking into a pair of warm brown eyes instead.

I'd never met this man before, but the bounce in his step and his handsome face piqued my curiosity. As the evening progressed, I kept finding myself glancing his direction. After the Bible study ended, the brown-eyed man made his way through the gathering and extended a large hand to shake mine. He said he'd moved from Boston a few weeks earlier and was looking forward to making some new friends in Florida. It was a short but enjoyable interaction. When I left that night, I wondered when I would see Matthew Vacaro again.

Although it had been several months since I'd dated anyone seriously, I was also coming off a string of short-term flings. In the past, I had always been more conservative about dating. Before my big breakup, I asked every suitor to speak with my dad before asking me out on a date. I considered any resulting relationship to be a courtship, with marriage as the ultimate goal. I didn't date casually, and I disliked dating culture in general.

After my recent heartbreak, however, I was done with doing things "the right way." I threw caution to the wind and decided to date just for fun. Every time a guy asked me out, I said yes. I started going on dates on a regular basis, regardless of whether I thought the guy was a viable candidate for marriage. I never went on more than one or two dates with anyone. Though I didn't compromise my physical standards, I almost completely ignored my old convictions about dating.

Then I met Matt.

I knew right away that I was interested in this tall, handsome man from Boston. After the Monday-night Bible study, we started crossing paths regularly, from chance encounters around town to movie nights with mutual friends. After a while, group interactions became one-on-one conversations, and one-on-one conversations turned into hours of texting. A wonderful friendship developed, and our feelings for each other started to blossom.

Selena's Quiet-Time Story

I have a hard time transferring my thoughts and feelings into words sometimes. It helps to remember that the Holy Spirit is our intercessor, so we don't always need to put our requests and feelings into just the right words. Recently I was reading Psalm 61 and thinking about how David was confident in the promises of the Lord even when he was facing hardship. Shortly after I read this passage, my husband told me that he had fallen into a past addiction again. As I was feeling defeated and broken down, the Holy Spirit brought to mind the words of Scripture: "I call as my heart grows faint; lead me to the rock that is higher than I. For you have been my refuge, a strong tower against the foe" (Psalm 61:2-3). I was reminded that God will sustain me—he will give me the rest and strength I need to move forward. I take comfort from knowing God always answers my prayers. Not always in the way I want, but I know he hears and answers.

Although we knew we liked each other, we also realized that the timing couldn't be worse. Matt was transitioning from a big move and didn't feel ready to date anyone. I was still recovering from a deeply hurtful breakup, and I was starting to feel convicted about my recent dating habits. Basically, we both sensed that the Holy Spirit was urging us to wait and take our relationship slowly. So one evening, after talking and praying it over, Matt and I agreed that it was best to just remain friends for now.

A few days later, we started dating anyway.

Instead of submitting to what I knew God had put on our hearts, I put the Lord's guidance out of mind. I wanted to hold hands and go on dates and call Matt my boyfriend more than I wanted to wait and trust the Lord's timing in this area of my life. So we impulsively plowed ahead. We figured we'd just have fun dating, no strings attached.

It didn't take long, though, before we realized our mistake. As soon as we went from being "just friends" to being boyfriend and girlfriend, the fragile bud of our new friendship was crushed under the weight of romantic expectations. Soon our interactions became strained and awkward. Matt wasn't sure he was ready to commit to an intentional relationship; meanwhile, I was more than ready to end my spree of purposeless dating. Eventually, the tension became too much, and after just four weeks, our short-lived romance ended.

After we broke up, I thought I would never see Matt again. I felt an intense wave of sadness as I realized what this mistake had cost me. Not only had I disregarded the Lord's nudging in my heart to wait before dating Matt, but I had also lost a good friend.

Our Helper

"Listen to your heart."

It's advice I've heard countless times—from movies, books, advertisements, and social media posts. When doubts arise or the way forward becomes unclear, we're taught that our most reliable guide can be found inside ourselves. We're encouraged to trust this "inner voice" or gut instinct above all else.

We didn't realize it at the time, but this "listen to your heart" attitude was what led Matt and me to start dating in the first place. Rather than taking the Holy Spirit's promptings seriously, we decided to go with our impulses. It's not surprising that this decision-making strategy let us down, since feelings and desires on their own are a poor guide for decision making. While your gut can lead you to choose one job over another, it can also convince you to steal from your boss. An inner impulse might prompt you to marry the love of your life, but that same impulse can later urge you to commit adultery. Even a murderer kills because it feels right.

Thanks to Jesus, we have a better guide available to us than our own deceitful hearts. As soon as we give our allegiance to Christ, we have the Holy Spirit living inside us. The more we read our Bibles and pray and get advice from trusted believers, the more the Holy Spirit will transform our hearts—including our "gut instincts."

The Holy Spirit is always at work in the lives of believers. He has our best interests at heart and is committed to helping us please the Father and bring glory to Jesus Christ. Thanks to him, we have access to wisdom for every decision and every interaction. The Holy Spirit is so helpful to us that Jesus told his disciples that it would be better for him to depart so the Holy Spirit could be with us (see John 16:7).

Here is a sampling of the work the Holy Spirit does in our lives:

- guides us into all truth (see John 16:13; 1 John 5:6)
- leads us to put sin to death (see Romans 8:13)
- prays for us according to God's perfect will (see Romans 8:26)
- transforms our hearts to be born again (see John 3:5-8)
- reveals Jesus to us (see Hebrews 10:15)
- spreads God's love in our hearts (see Romans 5:5)
- helps us testify about Jesus to others, especially our persecutors (see Luke 12:12)
- gives us gifts to strengthen other believers (see 1 Corinthians 12–14)
- leads us to explain God's Word to other people (see Acts 8:26-40)
- strengthens us to die courageously for Christ, if the occasion arises (see Acts 7:54-60)

It's important for every believer in Christ to cultivate an awareness of the Holy Spirit's leading. But the Holy Spirit won't force himself on us; it's our responsibility to listen for his voice. Paul urged the Ephesian believers to not grieve the Holy Spirit (see Ephesians 4:30), which indicates we can actively oppose or deliberately ignore his guidance. This is what I was doing on my little dating spree. If we aren't mindful of God's direction, we may end up listening to the enemy's lies instead.

God's Voice vs. Our Voice

So how can we tell the difference between the Holy Spirit and our own sinful nature?

We start with God's Word. The voice of the Spirit never contradicts the truth found in Scripture, and his leading is always in alignment with what

Glenda's Quiet-Time Story

When I was a young mom, it was difficult to have a consistent quiet time. I am an empty nester now, and I have plenty of time. I sense the Holy Spirit gently calling me into his presence daily. He never condemns me when I don't choose to spend time with him, but I know I am the one missing out! I don't want to miss all he has for me that day. When I choose to push through the difficulties of life and spend time with him, I am blessed by his closeness. He sits right with me, word after word, as I read Scripture. His Spirit encourages and convicts me. He never rushes me as I ponder his words to me; instead, he lovingly opens my eyes to see him more clearly.

we know of God's character as revealed in Scripture. Also, the Holy Spirit always seeks to bring glory to Christ. He will never lead us to do something that goes against God's desire.

The voice of sin, on the other hand, is prideful, self-glorifying, and narcissistic. It encourages us to lean on our own wisdom and put our hope in our own understanding. It diminishes others, obscures truth, demands instant gratification, resists self-sacrifice, and prioritizes momentary pleasure at the expense of eternal good. Listening to the voice of sin leads to disappointment and pain, because our wisdom can never compare with the Lord's.

As believers, we have two factions warring inside us: our sinful nature and the Holy Spirit. Ultimately, the voice we obey most will become the voice we hear the loudest. Every time we listen to and obey the leading of the Holy Spirit, his voice grows a little louder in our hearts. But every time we choose to ignore him, his voice grows more muted.

––––––––––

My breakup with Matt was a painful lesson in the importance of submitting to God's presence and guidance in all areas of my life. I had followed my heart's desire instead of the guidance of the Holy Spirit.

In the days after our breakup, I began to pray and confess my disregard for the Holy Spirit's cautions. As I did, I began to notice other areas in my life where I'd neglected listening to his voice. In my self-reliance, I was ignoring the helper that Jesus had sent to live in me. Even though I was having regular quiet times, the truth was that I didn't really want to be guided by him.

Submitting Our Quiet Time to the Holy Spirit

Just because we read the Bible and pray doesn't mean we're doing these activities in the right spirit. It's entirely possible for us to come before God in self-reliance and pride instead of humble dependence on him. Unless we submit ourselves to God, the motions of our quiet time may distract us from our relationship with the Lord himself.

In order to avoid hardness of heart, we must make the Holy Spirit an active participant in our daily Bible reading and prayer. This may seem obvious, yet it's something we're prone to forget. As we seek to welcome the Lord into our quiet time, it's important to distinguish between a Spirit-led quiet time and a flesh-led quiet time. Here are a few ways to recognize the difference.

Rigid vs. Flexible

While it's important to have a plan for spending time with Jesus, this plan can become an idol in our hearts. We are prone to turning good things into god things, and it's easy to prize our quiet-time routine as the ultimate goal rather than a close relationship with the Lord. This leads to a rigidity that is motivated by legalism rather than joy.

As someone who thrives on plans and schedules, I often

feel completely thrown off when unforeseen circumstances derail my agenda. This was true about my quiet time too. If something disrupted my time with the Lord, I would find myself resenting the person or circumstance that caused the interruption. This was a clear symptom of a flesh-led quiet time.

Thankfully God opened my eyes to the lack of grace in my quiet time. Eventually I realized that God does not follow my agenda. I need to be willing to adjust according to his Spirit's leading, even when my plans are disrupted.

> *Having a quiet time is about meeting with Jesus, not performing the exact right steps at the exact right time every single day!*

That doesn't mean I give up on the idea of sticking to a habit, but when my plans are derailed, I can, by God's grace, respond in joy and peace.

Having a quiet time is about meeting with Jesus, not performing the exact right steps at the exact right time every single day! Just as we glorify God by creating daily rhythms of Bible reading and prayer, we also glorify him by responding in patience when those rhythms get upended.

Self-Focused vs. Loving

People come before to-do lists. This may sound obvious, but it's easy to slip into a flesh-led quiet time and forget this truth.

Richard Shelley Taylor gives an excellent example of how

we can selfishly prioritize spiritual disciplines at the expense of those around us.

> An evangelist observed fasting on Wednesday and Friday for many years without variation under any circumstances. After several months of absence he came home to an eager, Daddy-hungry family. When they excitedly sat down to eat, the first meal as an unbroken family circle in all that time, he returned thanks, then left the table and shut himself in his room; it was his fast day. The gloom of disappointment settled down on the uncomprehending children. From one standpoint that would appear to be heroic self-denial. I am wondering if it was not rather a slavish bondage to habit. Even if self-denial was present, it is certain that in a still larger measure family-denial was present also. A higher discipline would have scorned the tyranny of petty rule and would have dictated eating with this wife and children a happy, hearty meal, then resuming the routine of fasting when he left for the next revival.[7]

The habit of a quiet time exists to glorify God and show love to others. As soon as our love for those around us is neglected because of a spiritual routine, the habit itself should take a back seat.

Through his example, Jesus showed us how to graciously respond to interruptions. Here are just two examples:

> Rising very early in the morning, while it was still dark, he departed and went out to a desolate place, and there he prayed. And Simon and those who were with him searched for him, and they found him and said to him, "Everyone is looking for you." And he said to them, "Let us go on to the next towns, that I may preach there also, for that is why I came out." And he went throughout all Galilee, preaching in their synagogues and casting out demons.
>
> MARK 1:35-39, ESV

> They went away in the boat to a desolate place by themselves. Now many saw them going and recognized them, and they ran there on foot from all the towns and got there ahead of them. When he went ashore he saw a great crowd, and he had compassion on them, because they were like sheep without a shepherd. And he began to teach them many things.
>
> MARK 6:32-34, ESV

In both of these instances, Jesus allowed his quiet time to be interrupted by the needs of others. Instead of shooing people away for the sake of prayer, Jesus had compassion, adjusted his plans, and took time to serve those around him.

Sometimes loving someone means changing or postponing our quiet time for the day. This is especially true for mothers of young children, who are interrupted countless times throughout the day by screaming infants, rambunctious toddlers, and hungry children. It's also true for caregivers, whose days are broken up by another person's needs, and for people with chronic illnesses, who aren't able to predict when they'll be interrupted by a health setback. Instead of feeling defeated and discouraged that our quiet times never seem to happen as planned, we can think of Jesus' example and be assured that these interruptions are simply another way of loving others and glorifying God.

> *Interruptions are simply another way of loving others and glorifying God.*

Demanding vs. Surrendered

Another key difference between a flesh-led and a Spirit-led quiet time is whether our attitude is marked by demanding from God or surrendering to God.

Are we coming to our quiet time with specific expectations of God? I don't mean the expectations that are based on the teachings of Scripture, such as the assurance that God loves us and hears each of our prayers. But are we expecting God to instantly change our feelings or our circumstances when we pray? Are we expecting him to answer our prayers in one specific way? These expectations reveal that we're approaching God with an attitude of "my will be done" instead of "thy will be done."

When I'm feeling physically tired or spiritually drained, it's tempting to think that the "fix" I need is having my quiet time—as though the act of reading my Bible and praying will magically send away all my negative feelings. While there's nothing wrong with humbly asking God to grant us peace and relieve our burdens, we shouldn't enter our time with him demanding that he do exactly what we wish. His knowledge and ways of working are superior to our own, so when we meet with him, we need to remember who he is and who we are. This helps us to approach him with a surrendered, humble heart.

A Redeemed Love Story

It had been months since I'd seen Matt.

The pain from our disobedience to the Lord's guidance and our subsequent breakup was still fresh, and my heart continued to ache over the friendship I'd lost. I couldn't quite put my finger on it, but I had a feeling that I'd lost something exceedingly precious. I had long since given up on the idea that Matt and I would be friends again.

Then, as subtly as a spring breeze, God began to bring Matt back into my life. I started seeing him at group gatherings, Bible studies, and movie nights. We made eye contact across the room again. We started to talk freely and laugh together. Eventually the tension between us melted into a renewed friendship.

Shortly after this fresh start, my mom found out that

Matt would be by himself for Christmas. She just couldn't bear the thought of him being alone in his apartment over the holidays, so she insisted on inviting him to our family's Christmas. To my surprise, Matt accepted my mom's invitation. He spent several days with us, getting to know my family and joining our games and traditions. Matt fit right in.

At first I was on guard. I didn't want to jump ahead of the Holy Spirit like I did the last time. Besides, I had a trip planned to photograph a wedding and visit friends. I was scheduled to leave for Thailand the day after Christmas, and I would be gone for almost a month. So when I left, I decided to leave behind any rekindled feelings for Matthew Vacaro too.

The morning after I arrived at my friend's house in Thailand, however, I checked my Facebook messages. There was a note from Matt waiting for me. Even though I'd been determined to forget all about him while I was away, I couldn't help but grin when I saw his message. I savored every word and wrote him back right away.

So began an online correspondence that lasted the entire month I was in Asia. Every day I would return from my activities to read Matt's messages, and as our conversations deepened, we began to truly get to know each other. We shared childhood memories, exposed our deepest fears, and expressed the things we loved about the Lord and following Jesus. With each message, my heart grew more hopeful that the Lord had something in store for Matt and me. This time, I was careful to be mindful of the Lord's guidance.

I didn't know it at the time, but Matt felt the same way. Every night after he got home from work, he would send me a message and then turn in for the night. He began to pray about what a possible future with me could look like.

The day I returned from Thailand, Matt met me and took me out for lunch. We ended up spending the rest of the day together, and when Matt dropped me off that night, he told me that he'd been praying about our relationship. He shared that he'd dreamed about me every night while I was away and sensed the Lord was prompting him to pursue me with the intention of marriage. He confided that the timing had been all wrong when we'd tried dating before, but now he was confident about the Lord's leading.

Words can't even express the joy I felt! Not only had I regained my dear friend, but this time we were seeking God's will for us.

At my request, Matt spoke with my dad, and we officially started dating. A year later, Matt took me to the spot in the church courtyard where we'd first met, pulled a ring out of his pocket, and got down on one knee.

Our Ever-Present Help

We are in need of help in every area of our lives—our relationships, our work, our decisions, our time with him. The good news is that we are not left to face any situation alone; God has given us his presence in the form of the Holy Spirit. He not only shows us what's right but also gives us the desire and the ability to do what's pleasing to him. Because of the Holy Spirit's work in us, we have the grace and freedom to say no to sin and yes to Jesus.

As with any skill, being mindful of God's presence and honoring his leading takes practice. It starts with the decision to surrender to his voice and to welcome him into every area of our lives. Of course, even with our best efforts and the help of the Spirit, we won't always get it right. Yet as my love story with Matt has *God loves redeeming the messes we make.* taught me, God is gracious and merciful when we blow it. He loves redeeming the messes we make. He wants us to keep coming back to him and seeking his help, no matter how many times we fail. The choice is ours, and the power is all his.

your turn

Read

John 14:15-31

Reflect

1. What parts of your life do you struggle to submit to the Holy Spirit? Why are you tempted to cling to those areas so tightly? .

2. Which of these flesh-led characteristics describes your quiet time: rigid, self-focused, or demanding? What would it look like for your time with Jesus to be more flexible, loving, and surrendered?

Grow

1. Make a list of decisions you want to surrender to the Lord's leading. Take time to pray over your list this week.

2. Make a list of relationships you want to surrender to the Lord's leading. Take time to pray over this list this week too.

Pray

Dear Jesus, thank you for sending us a helper, your Holy Spirit. Thank you for giving us the comfort, wisdom, and power to live as your followers in this world. Please help me to submit to the guidance of your Spirit in every area of my life. I especially want to rely on the Holy Spirit for _____. May my quiet time with you be flexible, surrendered, and loving. I'm so thankful that you are right here with me, and I want to enjoy your presence every single day. Amen.

changing seasons

Adapting Our Quiet Times to Our Circumstances

MATT AND I GOT MARRIED ON a beautiful October day out-side of Boston. We then spent our honeymoon enjoying the changing leaves and autumn colors in the White Mountains of New Hampshire. Unfortunately, our trip got off to a rocky start—quite literally.

The first day, we decided to hike a mountain, and as we crossed a small waterfall, we both slipped and fell down the rock face. I'll never forget my feeling of panic as the current took us over the waterfall and dumped us into a pool of ice-cold mountain water. Thankfully, we were unhurt apart from some bumps and bruises—and a cold walk back down the mountain. Later, as we warmed up by our cabin's fireplace, we joked that hopefully this "rocky start" wasn't a sign of what our future marriage would be like!

A week later we returned to Matt's parents' home in Massachusetts before heading back to Florida. Although they laughed along with us at the waterfall story, we could tell something heavy was hanging in the air. At dinner that night, Matt's mom shared that she had stage 1 breast cancer. She'd gotten the diagnosis right before our wedding but had waited to tell us, not wanting to diminish our joy.

We were stunned. No words seemed adequate for this news, and I could only watch as my husband wept in his mother's arms. The joy of our marriage had collided all too quickly with the harsh reality of our broken world.

We flew to Florida the next day and began to settle into our new life together. We unpacked our suitcases, washed our laundry, and organized our new apartment, still reeling from the news about Matt's mom.

Early one Wednesday morning, less than a week after we had returned from our honeymoon, my phone rang. Matt had left for work just a few minutes earlier. Why was he calling so soon?

"Hey, Matt! What's up?"

"Hey, babe." His voice was trembling. "So, I just got into a car accident."

Worst-case scenarios began to flash through my mind, but I tried to remind myself that he must be okay if he was talking with me on the phone. Thankfully, Matt was fine, as was the other party involved in the crash. His car, however, was not so fortunate.

Thirty minutes later, Matt returned to the apartment, sat on the couch, and put his head in his hands. His car had been totaled and was being towed away. It was a miracle that both he and the girl he hit were both unscratched, especially given the damage that had been done to their cars. We sat in stillness for a long time as I silently thanked God for his protection.

It wasn't the newlywed year we were anticipating. Matt's mom was treated for breast cancer and eventually beat it. God also provided a car for us after the accident. Even as we praised God for these answers to our prayers, we started to face other difficulties. Matt's job was stressful, and I was beginning to burn out from my own work as a wedding photographer. We were also struggling in our relationship.

Kira's Quiet-Time Story

Being a freshman in college has been a huge change for me. There are new responsibilities, new schedules, and new things to learn. This has put a damper on my quiet time. I get so distracted that I forget it was God who got me here in the first place. I'm still trying to adapt my routines and make God a priority in my life above all else. I usually have my quiet time in my dorm room. Once in a while I go to the third floor of our campus library to an open area with lots of windows and comfy chairs. I'll have my quiet time there, overlooking a beautiful lake. I want to have God constantly in my thoughts. Sometimes I talk to God in my head and have conversations with him about so many random things. I know he hears me and is always with me.

Our sin and selfishness were becoming more obvious now that we were married, and I was consistently stunned by my inability to sufficiently love my new husband. As much as we enjoyed being together, we also argued, cried, and wrestled through many challenges during those first months.

I also noticed that being married was affecting my quiet time. When I was single, I would read the Bible and pray every day. I was used to waking up alone and having mornings and evenings to myself. Now that I was married, I was barely squeezing in a quiet time once or twice a week. I felt disconnected from God, weak in my spiritual disciplines, and frustrated with my inability to adjust to these new circumstances.

I knew marriage would be a challenge, but I didn't realize just how much a new life phase would affect my relationship with the Lord. Eventually it became clear that I would need to completely relearn the habit of a quiet time—this time as a married woman.

Different Seasons, Different Quiet Times

We will all face new seasons at some point, whether it's moving to a new place, enrolling in classes, starting a new job, getting married, or having children. These new life circumstances can derail our daily routines, including our quiet time. It can be discouraging to watch our spiritual disciplines fall apart seemingly overnight.

In the midst of a transition, it helps to remember why

regular Bible reading and prayer are so important. The "how" of a quiet time may change over the years, but the "why" stays the same. When we keep in mind that spending time with Jesus is all about growing closer to him, we will be able to gracefully adapt our routines to fit the season we're in.

Although the specific circumstances will vary, we all go through transitions that impact our quiet time. As I look back over my life, there are a few key life stages that prompted a change in my routine. Of course, there's no "one size fits all" when it comes to time with Jesus, but perhaps you'll be able to resonate with some of my struggles and the lessons I've learned along the way.

High School

In high school, my responsibilities were limited, my schedule was flexible, and most of my needs were taken care of by my parents. This meant I was able to spend time reading my Bible and praying in the morning and then start my home-school assignments when I was done.

I realize that not everyone has the flexibility of a home-school education. If you attend public or private high school, you likely have a rigorous schedule and a heavy workload. Add in extracurricular activities, and free time becomes even more scarce. Having a daily quiet time when you're in high school can almost feel like extra homework, which makes it a difficult habit to develop. That's why, in my opinion, the best way to maintain a rhythm of Bible reading and prayer in this stage is to keep it simple.

Instead of structuring your quiet time around a list of goals, you can make it time oriented instead. For example, you might decide to spend fifteen to thirty minutes meeting with Jesus. Then you can evaluate how much time you want to spend reading, praying, or journaling and set your alarm. You could also try bringing your Bible to school and reading it over lunch or during breaks between classes. If you are a homeschooler like I was, try to savor the time and the freedom you have. Challenge yourself to read and study the Bible, establishing it as a habit in your life.

No matter what your high school experience looks like, the need for a quiet time remains the same. Our need for God doesn't diminish as our schedules fill up. If we train ourselves to depend on the Lord when we're young, it will be easier to do so later in life when even more responsibilities get added.

College/Early 20s

The years after high school represent some of the most significant changes we experience. During this transitional period, we transform from dependent minors to independent adults responsible for our own decisions.

Up to this point, you have probably been dependent on others to meet your basic needs. Your parents or other guardians have provided you with food, shelter, and clothing, along with guidelines for how to act morally. But a moment comes, whether at college or otherwise, when you are no longer considered a child. When that moment arrives, you hold in your hands the power to decide how you want to live.

This transition to living away from home is especially significant if you grew up in a Christian home, because once you leave, you are no longer obligated to practice your parents' faith. At this stage, it's up to you to decide whether you will walk away from your home-grown faith or if your faith will be solidified. Will you quit your walk with God, or will you bring yourself to face the hard questions and claim your faith for yourself?

Maybe having a quiet time was more your parents' idea than your own during high school, but once you step into independence, those routines can either change for the better or be dropped altogether. It no longer works to read the Bible and pray just because your parents told you to. Now it's up to you to do it because you want to.

If you decide to continue following Jesus as an independent adult, then Bible reading

Tristany's Quiet-Time Story

I'm finishing college and beginning my career, and between work, school, and other obligations, it's hard to find enough time to read and study God's Word as much as I'd like to. A verse that has been especially meaningful to me over the past several years is Psalm 73:26: "My flesh and my heart may fail, but God is the strength of my heart and my portion forever" (ESV). My body and my heart fail all the time. There are times when I don't read my Bible, and there are times when I read it just to check off a box. There are times I forget to pray, and there are times when I only pray about the things I want in life. There are times when I do what Scripture commands me not to do, and there are times when I don't do what it commands me to do. But this verse reminds me that God is still gracious and faithful. He never leaves me or forsakes me, and he gives me the strength I need to obey him.

and prayer should continue as a regular rhythm in your life. If you're in college, with a heavy class load, work responsibilities, and a new social life to cultivate, it can be challenging to stick with a quiet-time routine. You might try waking up early enough to have a quiet time before your classes. Another possibility is to finish your assignments at a reasonable hour in the evenings so you can spend time with Jesus before going to bed. It may be necessary to say no to some activities on campus if you want to maintain a regular quiet time.

Life is full of new freedoms and responsibilities in the years following high school, and it's easy for your quiet time to end up on the back burner. But you need the Lord now more than ever!

Career

Another huge transition is entering the work force. For the first time, school is behind you, and you enter the working world. This can be an incredibly jarring transition if you're used to an ever-changing class schedule. All at once you're accountable to an employer, you have a limited number of hours at home, and you have only a handful of vacation days to enjoy throughout the year.

The new freedom you discovered after leaving home almost feels as though it has been lost again in the daily grind of work, and this can come as quite a shock. Instead of being accountable to the rules of a household, you are now bound to please your boss or supervisor. Instead of being taken care of by your parents, you assume responsibility for rent, bills, and other financial obligations.

Your quiet time can be greatly disrupted by this transition, mainly because it's overwhelming to work forty hours every week at a new (and likely demanding) job. Learning the ropes of a new role takes time, and it's tempting to put all your energy and focus into your new career responsibilities and leave your quiet time behind.

However, the consistency of a job can actually benefit your quiet time. Chances are, you have a little more predictability in your schedule, and you probably know your work hours in advance. This allows you to choose a time for Bible reading and prayer, and then stick with it.

I came to realize two things about my schedule during this season. First, my social life took place mainly in the evenings after work, and second, my workday started at a strict time each morning. This meant that if I wanted to have a consistent quiet time, I needed to sacrifice my love of sleeping by waking up early enough to read my Bible and pray before work. Although it took some perseverance, I saw this as an opportunity to cement my quiet-time habit in place.

Marriage

The transition from being single to married also has the potential to throw your quiet time way off. Before Matt and I got married, people told us marriage would be hard, so we walked into our vows bracing for the worst. We had our fair share of struggles, disagreements, and disappointments, but marriage wasn't as hard as either of us expected. My quiet time, however, took a huge hit after I got married. The biggest challenge for me was the lack of privacy.

Until that point, I hadn't realized how much I'd relied on solitude in order to have a "successful" quiet time. Before getting married, I was able to wake up on my own, pray out loud, and walk around with my Bible in hand. At night I would often lie alone in the darkness of my room and talk to Jesus. Occasionally I would even dance to worship music with the lights off.

I stopped doing these things as soon as I married Matt.

I went from spending time with Jesus every day to reading my Bible only once or twice a week. *What's wrong with me?* I wondered. Why was it suddenly so hard to spend time with Jesus? Was my quiet-time struggle evidence that I'd made my husband an idol?

In my typical fashion, I attempted to pick apart all the reasons this was happening, jumping to the worst possible conclusions about my faith. Over time I began to realize that my struggle wasn't necessarily evidence of a deeper spiritual issue; rather, I was clinging to the form of quiet time instead of its function: to spend time with Jesus.

I had become so settled in the motions of my routine that when I needed to be flexible, I forgot all about why I was having a quiet time in the first place. The important thing was meeting with Jesus, and I didn't have to be alone, quiet, or perfectly situated in an armchair to do that. Instead, I just had to come to him, as imperfect as my attempt might be.

With this new perspective, I was able to adjust my quiet

time. I was used to reading the Word around six or seven in the morning, but why couldn't I come before the Lord at ten o'clock instead? So I started meeting with Jesus later in the morning, when Matt was at work. When he was home, I would write out my prayers instead of praying aloud like I used to. At first it felt strange, but these adaptations eventually became enjoyable—and even the new normal for my quiet time.

Even though your quiet time might change, God's love for you never does.

If you are newly married and struggling with your quiet-time routine, remember: it doesn't matter how you come to Jesus; it just matters that you *do* come to him! It may feel awkward to have your quiet time in front of your spouse, but time with Jesus is worth it, and it will eventually get more comfortable. It might also be motivating to your spouse to see you practicing a regular quiet time.

So give yourself time and patience as you adjust to being married. It may take months to find your new quiet-time rhythm, and that's okay! Don't give up, get creative, and trust that even though your quiet time might have to change, God's love for you never does.

Motherhood

On September 30, 2020, I gave birth to my first baby. It was a day Matt and I had been eagerly preparing for, and I'll never forget the adrenaline and excitement that filled us as we timed contractions on our way to the hospital. Cove arrived after fourteen hours of labor, and in that moment, our lives were transformed.

The days after Cove's birth were a fog of sweetness and exhaustion. We were thrilled to be parents and relieved that the long wait was over. However, almost as soon as we arrived home from the hospital, our euphoria was replaced by the bleary-eyed feeling of being completely overwhelmed.

Neither Matt nor I knew how to take care of a nine-pound baby human. Cove was an utterly strange creature, full of demands that we didn't know how to properly fulfill. We stumbled our way through diaper changes and baths, fingernail clippings and nighttime nursing sessions. We struggled to swaddle his flailing arms, calm his frantic cries, and support his little head. We would solve one problem just as another perplexing stage of babyhood began.

As the weeks passed, we started thanking God for the smallest of victories, like being able to take a shower or go on a walk with Cove in the stroller. When Matt returned to work, I was faced with balancing the responsibilities of home, a business, and a newborn baby all at the same time.

That's when my quiet time became almost nonexistent.

Most days I was too tired to read the Bible. Taking the time to pray felt nearly impossible, and journaling was a luxury I could no longer afford. My only moments of quiet happened while Cove took naps, and he rarely napped long enough for me to have my typical hour with the Lord. In order to resuscitate my habit of daily devotions, I had to get creative. I did this by putting my Bible and journal on the shelf and turning to other tools instead.

I started listening to the Bible on my phone while I washed dishes, folded laundry, or played with the baby. I started praying while I was nursing and getting on my knees for a few minutes before Cove woke up from his naps. My quiet time hovered in survival mode for the first several months of his life.

I don't think I'm alone in this struggle. The truth is, being a mother, especially of little ones, is more than a full-time job. It is a 24/7 demand for your attention. The younger your children are, the more hands-on your mothering needs to be. It's not that downtime doesn't exist at all; rather, it's that quiet moments are far outnumbered by the demands of your to-do list.

As soon as the baby goes down for a nap, you can choose between ten different items that all need to be done. Laundry needs to be folded, dishes need to be washed, floors need to be swept, emails need to be responded to, groceries need to be bought, budgets need to be balanced, and plants need to be watered, along with dozens of other time-consuming tasks. It's a race to complete what you can before the baby wakes up.

The decision to sit down and pray feels much costlier when you become a mother, especially when time spent with Jesus could be used for showering or taking a much-needed nap. Nevertheless, communing with the Lord in some form needs to be a top priority for mothers, because casting our cares on him is just as necessary as showering every day. Being a mom is harder when we neglect our spiritual needs. So it really is better for the dishes to be delayed or the laundry to be temporarily set aside than it is for our souls to be left untended. Time with Christ, though difficult and costly, is essential, especially when we're knee deep in the trenches of motherhood.

When we're feeling overwhelmed by everything that's competing for our attention, it helps to remember that this season won't last forever. Time might be scarce with a newborn, but soon that baby will sleep on a more consistent schedule and be more capable of self-entertaining. One day they may even be able to help watch younger siblings! At some point, children can be trained to remain in their bedrooms until a certain time so you can spend some uninterrupted moments with Jesus, or they can be taught to have their own quiet time while you have yours. The form may change as your children grow up; the important thing is not to forsake Bible reading and prayer altogether.

Our children need us to seek Jesus.

It also helps to remember that we don't spend time with Jesus solely for our own benefit. *Our children need us to seek Jesus.* They need us to have our cups filled by the water of life, and they need to witness our example as we make it a priority to daily meet with our Creator. The truth is, only God's grace can transform an overwhelmed mother into a peaceful, patient, joyful caregiver. So let's look to him in faith every day to do just that.

Avoiding Comparison

One of the greatest sources of quiet-time discouragement is comparison. I'm not talking about the good kind of comparison—the type that inspires you to imitate someone else's maturity and faithfulness. Unhealthy comparison results in self-pity, frustration, and self-focus. Not everyone is in the same season of life, and not everyone has the same personality or set of circumstances. Instead of feeling a sense of shame that we don't measure up, we need to humbly recognize and accept our own limitations.

We also shouldn't compare our current quiet-time season to a previous one. When I was a recent college graduate and starting my business as a wedding photographer, I was able to pray for an hour in my closet every day. I would light a candle, close the door, set my alarm for an hour, and just pray. It was one of the most enjoyable seasons I've ever spent in the Lord's presence. But it didn't last long! After a few months, my schedule and responsibilities changed again, and that hour of prayer slimmed down to ten minutes.

Now that I'm the mom of an infant with an unpredictable schedule, it's tempting to look back and pine for that prayer closet. I miss the luxury of having an uninterrupted hour all to myself! In reality, however, that season was no better than the one I'm in now. Jesus is no less my King in this life stage than he was then, and the same amount of grace covers my quiet time today. One day I'll have more margin again. In the meantime, obedience looks like full hands, a busy schedule, and limited time to read the Bible and pray.

Depending on your life stage, obedience may look like full hands, a busy schedule, and limited time to read the Bible and pray.

No matter what life stage we're in, it's the presence of Jesus we seek. He is faithful to meet the heart that genuinely seeks him, no matter what the circumstances look like.

your turn

Read

Psalm 23

Reflect

1. What season of life are you currently in? What is challenging about this season? What do you enjoy about this season?

2. How does your current life stage impact your ability to spend time with Jesus?

Grow

1. Make a timeline of your life, including the major life stages and transitions you've experienced. Beside each season, write a note or draw a picture that represents what your quiet time was like.

Pray

Dear Jesus, thank you for this season of _____. Thank you for knowing and holding every stage in your hand. You know the joys of this time, as well as the struggles and sorrows. Please remind me how desperately I need you during this (and every!) season. Help me to spend time with you and not to give up reading the Bible and praying, no matter what my circumstances are. Thank you for meeting me in times of peace, times of overwhelm, times of struggle, and times of blessing. Amen.

10

quiet time in community

Our Need for Christ-Centered Fellowship

"I JUST CAN'T SEEM TO MAKE IT HAPPEN."

We were sitting in my living room as the sun set, sipping tea and nibbling cookies. Every Thursday night at 7:00 p.m., five to ten women gathered in my living room for food, fellowship, and prayer as we caught up on life and left our burdens at the foot of the Cross. The faces around me ranged from late teens to early thirties. We were all in different seasons of life, but that night we were commiserating about the exact same struggle: having a daily quiet time.

"I mean, I try to spend time reading the Bible," my friend continued, "but for some reason the habit just won't stick!" Every head nodded in agreement, including my own. One by one, we shared about our quiet-time difficulties, past and present. It was a topic we hadn't talked about much before, but it was quickly becoming clear that disciplines like regular Bible reading and prayer were a challenge for all of us.

We encouraged and poured hope into one another, and we ended the evening in prayer, asking the Lord to help us maintain the regular habit of seeking him. We left feeling as if a burden had been lifted. We weren't alone in our struggle, and it seemed like a small victory to be able to share honestly in the context of our community.

That night I realized that I was not alone in the struggle to have a daily quiet time—this was a challenge for women in all stages of life. I didn't know it yet, but the Lord was planting seeds in my heart to do something about it.

One year later, I was sitting at my dining room table reading the Bible and praying. The view from our third-story apartment was uninspiring, to say the least, but I made up for it with a lit candle and a fresh cup of coffee. I'd been struggling to maintain my quiet-time rhythm since getting married, and that day I found my thoughts wandering as I reached across the table for my various journals and scraps of paper scribbled with prayer lists.

I'd been feeling discontented with my job in wedding photography for several months now, and the prayer that remained constantly on my lips was that the Lord would lead me wherever he wanted me to go. I was beginning to wonder if God wanted to change my life path along with my passions. Though I'd been praying about this for months, I hadn't sensed an answer.

On that rainy morning, however, something was different. In that moment, the Lord inspired me with an idea that would change the trajectory of my life.

As I gathered my journals, papers, note cards, and printouts, I wished in exasperation that I had something like a planner to keep my quiet time organized. As soon as the thought entered my mind, my heart began to race. Was there such a thing as a quiet-time planner? I immediately started researching. I scoured the internet to find something that wasn't just another journal but an actual planner and organizer where I could keep all my tools for seeking God. After a few

Jemila's Quiet-Time Story

Some of my greatest quiet-time victories have been when I spend time reading the Bible in community with other people! This is when I'm able to talk out my thoughts, get different perspectives, and celebrate the ways God is working in the lives of others. You don't need to be in a trendy coffee shop or have a theology degree to start reading Scripture. Open your Bible and begin letting God's Word breathe into your life. You will see a difference in your countenance and the way you handle yourself after spending daily quiet time with Jesus.

hours of looking, I'd found nothing close to what I wanted. I closed my computer, stood up, and said aloud to the empty room, "I'm going to make this thing myself!"

From that moment on, I got busy making my idea a reality. I called the planner the *Quiet Time Companion*. I pulled together a group of friends for advice, I searched for print manufacturers, and I invested the money I'd earned from shooting weddings to create the journals.

As the project started coming together, I began to realize that the *Quiet Time Companion* would only scratch the surface of my desire to help others in their quiet times. What I really wanted to do was create a community dedicated to encouraging and supporting women in their daily habit of seeking Jesus. I wanted to provide a place where they could be challenged, encouraged, and held accountable in Bible reading and prayer. It was around that time that I read Jeremiah 29:13: "You will seek me and find me, when you seek me with all your heart" (ESV). In that moment I knew what the name of this new ministry would be: Wholehearted.

In late 2018, my dream became a reality. The *Quiet Time Companion* was launched, along with the Wholehearted ministry. Soon we were sending planners to women all over the country and even the world. I gathered a team of writers for the Wholehearted blog and began sending a weekly email featuring stories of Christian women who had regular quiet times. Women from every walk of life started to discover Wholehearted, and the community began to grow. As women stepped out of their isolation and into our online community, we began to hear about real change in their lives.

Joining Community

> The LORD God said, "It is not good that the man
> should be alone; I will make him a helper fit for him."
> GENESIS 2:18, ESV

On the beginning pages of Scripture, we see a universal truth spoken from the lips of God: it is not good for man to be alone. This was the first time God looked at his creation and pronounced something "not good." Up to that point, everything he'd made was perfect. I have often thought that perhaps God delayed in creating Eve in order to make an eternally resonating point: human beings need to be in companionship with one another and ultimately with God himself.

God's trinitarian nature reflects this truth. The Father, Son, and Holy Spirit dwell in eternal, loving relationship with one another. Since it isn't possible for love to exist apart from a relationship, love began in this central relationship between the Father, the Son, and the Holy Spirit—a relationship that predates creation! As beings created in God's image, we, too, need companionship so we can give and receive love.

As beings created in God's image, we need companionship so we can give and receive love.

The trouble is, we live in a broken world, where sin attempts to destroy every good and harmonious relationship. Not only that, but we dwell in a culture where radical individualism is the religion of choice. Everything from advertisements to entertainment to education is obsessed with self. This "me first" mindset has infiltrated every part of our lives. When "me" instead of "we" becomes the focus of our lives, we break off from God's original design for loving companionship, and every kind of heartache ensues. Unfortunately, radical individualism has even taken hold in church culture.

It's true that God created us as individuals, and therefore it's important to value each human being for their unique gifts and needs. However, God intended us to use our gifts and have our needs met in the context of community. When our eyes are focused on others instead of ourselves, we begin to experience the lasting joy of Christlike love, which delights in self-denial. Jesus wants us to love one another the way he loved us. So when we place others' needs ahead of our own, we bear the fruit of a community in which love abounds.

So how do we find this community, especially in an age when radical individualism seems to control every aspect of life? As with most countercultural practices, we can't expect it to happen automatically; we must be ready to step forward and take the initiative. We begin by finding a local body of believers to gather with on a regular basis. Then we make an intentional effort to welcome the people sitting next to us in the pew into our homes and our lives. After all, we live life not in the church building but in our living rooms, around our dining room tables, and at our kitchen sinks. It is in the home where we pour out our hearts, laugh, weep, share stories, and experience fellowship. Meaningful community is elusive unless we're willing to invite others into our homes and enter their homes.

This may come as a surprise, but this need for Christian community also applies to our quiet times. While time with the Lord is a private habit, the practice should not be isolated from community. Just as fellow believers can help us move houses, watch kids, repent from sin, and be set free from our burdens, they can also help us create and keep the habit of seeking Jesus.

There are a few key ways we can grow in the Lord in community: by seeking accountability, by submitting to mentorship, and by asking the awkward questions.

Seeking Accountability

When we ask someone to hold us accountable, we are essentially humbling ourselves enough to reveal our sinful tendencies. We are giving another person the authority to keep tabs on us and, when necessary, to confront us in love. In other words, accountability means letting go of our right to privacy to make room for actual change.

Sin finds its power in darkness, denial, and deceit. So the more we hide our sin, the stronger it becomes and the harder it is to get the help we need. Transparency is one of the weapons God has given us to fight sin, as

> *Accountability means letting go of our right to privacy to make room for actual change.*

it allows us to shine the bright light of truth on what would otherwise remain hidden and lead to the destruction of our hearts, our relationships, and our lives. Though accountability like this is painful, it is ultimately what sets us free. Accountability is a nonnegotiable for the Christian who is serious about bearing fruit.

Accountability doesn't just happen on its own. It's awkward to dig into sin issues or spiritual struggles with fellow Christians. This is no surprise, since the pervading worldview is one of universal acceptance. To view anyone's behavior as wrong is seen as hateful and even bigoted. Our culture encourages women to be outspoken about our "mess," whether it's eating issues, anxiety, attitudes, or lack of discipline. At the same time, we're also told not to apologize for being "who we really are." This is akin to decorating someone's prison cell without encouraging them to walk out and be free. This way of thinking flies in the face of the Bible's central message that we *are* a mess and that we need God's forgiveness.

As the culture around us bends over backward to accept any and all lifestyles, believers will find it increasingly difficult to confront one another about sin in our lives. Seeking accountability for ourselves and offering it to others is radically countercultural. It's not enough to shake hands on a Sunday morning and engage in superficial chitchat. We need to be intentional about going deep with other believers—gathering with the intention of glorifying God and pointing one another to Christ. When we do, wounds are healed, chains are broken, prayers are answered, and eternity is moved.

Accountability is especially lacking when it comes to quiet time. While we might be vaguely encouraged to spend time with Jesus on a regular basis, it's rare to have specific people keeping us accountable. When I was younger, my quiet-time accountability partner was my mother. In more recent years, it has been my husband. They often ask me how I'm doing in Bible reading and prayer, and since they live in close proximity to me, they can tell when I'm struggling. Knowing there's someone who expects me to seek Jesus gives me extra motivation to stick with the habit. While this is uncomfortable at times, I know it's essential for keeping my wandering heart anchored to Christ.

If you're struggling with your quiet time and want to find someone to help keep you accountable, start by bringing this request to the Lord in prayer. Ask him to prepare the right person to help you walk this road. As you interact with women at your church, be bold in asking them out for coffee. If you sense that the person you're talking to is trustworthy and mature in her faith, don't be afraid to dive deep and reveal your true struggles. If she grows uncomfortable and distant, she wouldn't be a good fit as an accountability partner. However, if she's willing to discuss her own struggles along with yours, it's a good sign that this relationship is worth pursuing.

Once you've found an accountability partner, make a plan for meeting on a regular basis. Map out the aspects of your quiet times that you'll keep each other accountable to, and create a list of questions to ask each other on a weekly (or daily) basis, either in person or via text message. After you've made your plan, get started! Over time you may find that more people will want to join, creating a circle of accountability that will strengthen the faith of everyone involved.

If we belong to Christ, we need not fear the discomfort of accountability. Through his work on the cross, Jesus has taken away all our guilt and shame. His love breaks the power of fear that often comes with public confession and repentance. To accept Christ's grace is to acknowledge the worst about ourselves, so what do we have to hide? Sin no longer defines us, which means we are free to battle it with all our might as we rest in our identity as children of God.

Submitting to Mentorship

Another gift of Christian community is mentorship. A mentor is slightly different from an accountability partner, since this person is a few steps ahead in maturity and can teach us what they've learned along the way.

In Western culture, there has been a shift away from mentorship in the past few generations. It used to be that life skills were passed down from mothers to daughters, from fathers to sons, from seasoned Christians to new believers. Now personal autonomy is prized as supreme. People are eager for positions of leadership, while the art of modest followership is shunned. Where fathers once taught sons, young men now look up to celebrities and athletes. Where mothers once mentored daughters, there is now Google. It's more convenient to get our answers from the internet and pop culture, and besides, the older generations aren't held in the same esteem they once were.

For a Christian, however, there's a strong biblical case for submitting to a mentor. The apostle Peter writes that younger Christians ought to submit to the elders of their church (see 1 Peter 5:5). God's people are also commanded to treat older men and women with respect (see 1 Timothy 5:1-2; Leviticus 19:3, 32). Children are told to honor their parents (see Exodus 20:12). These mentors are a source of wisdom—we can learn from their experiences in the hope that we will continue their legacy of faithful obedience to the Lord (see Proverbs 6:20; 23:22; Ephesians 6:1-2).

Elizabeth's Quiet-Time Story

After my fourth child was born, I felt lost about jumping back into a quiet time—and frankly, just lost as a person. I said to my husband, "I wish I had someone to point me in the right direction." He suggested I talk to a woman from our church who had adult kids. I asked her if she would be interested in mentoring me. She said yes, and two and a half years later, she is now my best friend. She has taught me so much—not just what the Bible says but how to study it. I've grown so much because of her willingness to mentor me. And because of her mentorship and friendship, I am now mentoring a younger mom too.

In my own search for mentors, I look for someone whose character matches the standards Paul used to select church elders:

> Appoint elders in every town as I directed you—if anyone is above reproach, the husband of one wife, and his children are believers and not open to the charge of debauchery or insubordination. For an overseer, as God's steward, must be above reproach. He must not be arrogant or quick-tempered or a drunkard or violent or greedy for gain, but hospitable, a lover of good, self-controlled, upright, holy, and disciplined. He must hold firm to the trustworthy word as taught, so that he may be able to give instruction in sound doctrine and also to rebuke those who contradict it.
>
> TITUS 1:5-9, ESV

These standards reveal whether someone has submitted the entirety of their life to Christ. Are they faithful to their spouse? Do they raise their children to know and understand the gospel? Do they have self-control over their attitudes and habits? Do they love others through hospitality and good works? Do they pursue holiness and godly discipline? And most important, do they see God's Word as the ultimate authority over their life? This is the picture of a person who has experienced God's grace and is walking the road of sanctification into true maturity. Of course, even the most mature believer sins and makes mistakes, but when they do, they respond in humility and repentance. This is the kind of Christian we should strive to be—and it's the type of person to seek as a mentor.

I have been mentored by many godly women over the years. When I was younger, I was mentored by women on the mission field in Mongolia. When I moved to America, my host mother quickly became (and continues to be) a beloved mentor. Of all the women who have poured into my life, however, my own mother has always been the most influential. She has been my most consistent mentor, not only because she is related to me, but because she is the kind of Christ follower I want to be someday.

To find the right mentor, we need to be involved in a solid Christian community. The church you're a part of will likely determine the kind of mentor you get. If you are part of a body of believers that carefully values the teaching of God's Word and delights in knowing and worshiping the Lord, you are more likely to find a mentor who is capable of guiding you to maturity in the Christian faith.

Although spending time with an older mentor in real life is best, it may still be beneficial to find a mentor virtually. Depending on your life circumstances, it may not always be possible to learn from someone face-to-face. That's one of the reasons I created Wholehearted. I saw the need among women for help and encouragement in developing a quiet-time habit, and I realized that even though online encouragement isn't a substitute for an in-person mentor, it could be a help to some women. Joining a Christ-centered online community can encourage us to keep our relationship with Jesus in the forefront of our minds as we scroll, post, and consume content.

Another reason for finding a mentor, beyond maturing in our own faith, is to become mentors ourselves one day. The idea that all Christians should become teachers and mentors in the faith was the expectation from the beginning. The writer of the book of Hebrews admonishes believers for remaining immature for too long. He writes, "Though by this time you ought to be teachers, you need someone to teach you the elementary truths of God's word all over again" (Hebrews 5:12). The Lord expects us to mature in our faith, our knowledge of him, and our obedience to him so we'll be able to help others grow in their faith as well. Submitting ourselves to wise mentorship is one of the best ways to prepare for a future of helping others along the same road.

Asking the Awkward Questions

Whenever someone comes to me with a sin struggle, whether it's fear, lust, discontentment, gossip, envy, or something else, I always ask the same question: "Do you have a regular quiet time?"

It's not that you won't struggle with these sins if you spend time with God regularly, but if you've tried desperately to be set free and haven't prayed about it yet, then that's the place to start. If you're losing a battle against sin but haven't spent time filling yourself up with God's Word, that's the next step.

I've found that most Christians don't have many people in their lives who actively care about the time they spend with God. After all, it's kind of an awkward conversation. It may seem like the polite thing not to put someone on the spot when it comes to their time with the Lord, but in reality, we're not doing a friend any favors when we gloss over something that is so closely related to our spiritual health. I now usually ask my struggling friends the awkward questions since I might be the only one who does.

The point here is not how a quiet time helps us defeat our sin (though it certainly plays an important role!). Rather, the lesson is that we should be ready to help one another by explicitly asking if we are spending time with God regularly. We don't ask out of self-righteousness or a desire to make the other person uncomfortable; we ask because, by the grace of God, bringing this issue into the light might help our friends experience a breakthrough in their struggle with sin. It is within such honest communication that our community—and the relationships within it—becomes a force for transformation.

> *By God's grace, our community can be a force for transformation.*

Instead of offering detached sympathies and quick fixes, let's become intentional enough to ask our friends the awkward questions. It may feel intrusive, even offensive, but

197

if we don't ask, who will? Sometimes people are silently longing for someone to challenge and encourage them, and just asking how they're doing in their relationship with God gives them the opportunity to be honest about their struggle.

In an age of distraction and constant entertainment, it's easy to forget the true depth of a human soul. We are deep creatures, full of dreams, struggles, fears, failures, and longings. This means it's vital that we form Christian friendships that go beyond casual chitchat. In order to experience worthwhile community, we must be willing to break through to deeper levels to ask the hard questions. It may be messy at times, but it's the only way to truly care for one another the way Christ wants us to.

Although having a quiet time is a private practice, it's all the sweeter and more consequential when it's done in the context of community, accountability, and mentorship. When we start seeing ourselves as part of a community, we will begin to experience the sweetness of walking to the heavenly Kingdom with our fellow pilgrims. Within such Christ-centered companionship, our quiet times will start to thrive.

your turn

Read

Ecclesiastes 4:9-12; Hebrews 3:12-13; Titus 2:3-5

Reflect

1. How would you describe your community right now? Are there people in your life you can share authentically with? Are there people who love you enough to ask the awkward questions?

2. In what areas of your life are you in most need of accountability?

Grow

1. Write down the names of three of your closest friends. Do you enjoy Christ-centered fellowship with them? How could you deepen these relationships?

2. Write down a potential accountability partner and a possible mentor. Now reach out to each of them to see if they'd be interested in setting up a first meeting.

Pray

Dear Jesus, thank you for creating me to live in community with others. Thank you for your presence with me, and thank you for being my truest companion. Help me to love others the way you love me. Please bring me into a Christ-centered community, and help me to cultivate deep friendships. I also pray that you would lead me to the right accountability partners and mentors. Teach me how to be a humble follower, how to imitate the Christlike example of others, and how to be an example for those who come after me. Amen.

the ripple effect

Having a Quiet Time Impacts Everyone around Us

I COULD HARDLY BELIEVE MY EYES. Although my hand shook as I held the pregnancy test, there was no denying the result. It was positive!

I had a feeling I might be pregnant, but after about seven months of trying to conceive, Matt and I were trying to keep our expectations low. In that instant, however, everything changed. As I walked out of the bathroom and handed the test to my husband, tears of joy began to run down my face.

The first few days after finding out we were pregnant were filled with happiness and excitement. Almost immediately, we began dreaming about the future, planning for what our life would look like as a family of three, and praying for the healthy arrival of our firstborn child. Soon we began telling friends, sharing on social media, and ordering the gender-reveal cake that would announce that we were having a boy.

One day, about sixteen weeks into my pregnancy, I was sitting on our sofa having my quiet time when I felt a flutter of tiny kicks in my womb. Joy and awe washed over me as I realized there really was a human being growing inside me. That day I started to feel the true gravity of being a mother. I began to hope and pray that Matt and I would lead our children well and that we would leave a legacy that pointed them toward Christ.

As I prepared to welcome my firstborn, I realized that the best thing I could do to make my hopes a reality for my children was to maintain an intimate, daily relationship with Jesus myself. I knew this to be true because of the example my own mother set for me.

There has been no greater influence on my quiet-time routine than my mother. Most mornings during my childhood, I would wake up and sneak out of bed into the living room. I would be met with the same scene time after time: there was my mom, reading her Bible and praying.

When I was young, I assumed every adult spent time with Jesus the way my parents did. Eventually I realized how uncommon it is to have a mother who practices a regular quiet time. My mother's desire to treasure Jesus above everything, even her husband and children, led me to see that Jesus is worthy of my own adoration.

While there's no guarantee that our faithfulness to Christ

will result in others' faithfulness to him, there's no doubt in my mind that having a daily quiet time affects not only us but everyone around us.

Changing the World

Being a world changer is on trend. This is an attractive idea, especially when we've experienced the great rescue of Jesus. It's tempting to think that in order to effect change, we need to start *doing* more. Maybe volunteering is the key, or giving more money or serving more often or hosting more dinners in our home. While these practices are good and worthwhile, perhaps the best thing we can do to change the world is something that often goes overlooked: spending private time in the presence of Jesus.

Jesus transforms people's lives, which means spending time with him transforms us! It's impossible to consistently walk into the presence of a holy God and leave unchanged. Reading our Bibles and praying isn't just about getting a dose of good feelings for the rest of the day. We also get to experience sanctification as the Holy Spirit works in the hidden places of our lives to make us more like Christ.

It's impossible to consistently walk into the presence of a holy God and leave unchanged.

Of course, thanks to the Holy Spirit, we know that God is working on us even when we're not reading our Bible and praying. Yet it's this ongoing pattern of discipline that

> *The more we are with Jesus, the more we are transformed by him.*

opens the door to the Holy Spirit in every aspect of our lives. The more we are with Jesus, the more we are transformed by him. It doesn't end there though. Spending time with God eventually sends ripples to everything and everyone around us.

We are holistic people, made up of flesh and spirit, body and mind, heart and soul. The way we relate to God in private influences how we relate to others in public. It may not be obvious at first, but eventually our private devotion (or lack thereof) will be revealed. The seeds we plant today will be harvested tomorrow.

As we spend time with Jesus, our world will undoubtedly be changed, including our friendships, our workplaces, our marriages, and our children.

Quiet Time Affects Our Friendships

Nothing can compare to the joy of a solid friendship. Some of my favorite moments are those I've shared with my close friends, whether it's a deep conversation over an iced latte or a laughing fit during a ridiculous game.

God created friendship to provide us with companionship, protection, growth, admonishment, and encouragement as we make our way through this wonderful and sometimes woeful world. We were not made to live alone but to experience the delight of doing life hand in hand with others. Since friendship is so valuable, both to us and to our

Maker, it's wise for us to ensure the spiritual health of these relationships.

Believe it or not, having a regular quiet time is one of the best ways to help our friendships flourish. This is true for many reasons. First, when we strive to make Jesus our greatest joy and hope, we guard our friendships against becoming idolatrous—a tendency that can crush any relationship. But when our friendships remain secondary to Jesus, we (and our friends) can be ourselves, flaws and all.

Another benefit to having a regular quiet time is that it prepares us to deal with conflict. Friendships can get messy when our differences collide, especially if we respond to these differences sinfully. We're not always patient with our friends. We put our own interests above theirs. We don't always honor them in the way we talk to them or about them. We fall into bitterness, gossip, envy, and a myriad of other friendship-destroying attitudes. Every so often, we find that we have a broken relationship on our hands.

As we spend time with Jesus, our world will undoubtedly be changed.

Whenever sin damages one of my friendships, my instinct is to try to fix the problem on my own. Although I hate conflict and confrontation, I hate an unresolved issue even more. So when trouble seems to be brewing in one of my friendships, I often hurry to hash it out. Sometimes this tactic works, and sometimes it doesn't. When my efforts fail, I'm reminded that I have access to the one who created friendship in the first place.

As I spend time with Jesus, I can lay my broken friend-ships at his feet. When I'm struggling to love a friend or when I discover a judgmental or envious spirit within me, I've learned that the best way to kill off those sinful atti-tudes is to pray. I might struggle initially to find empathy, but if I keep praying for the person, my heart eventually melts toward them. This change doesn't happen right away, especially if the hurt is deep. But with time and the help of the Holy Spirit, bitterness is replaced by humility, love, and gratitude.

When we spend regular time with Jesus, we are also better prepared to encourage our friends by speaking the truth in love. Sometimes simply being with a friend who is struggling and listening to them is the best way to help. But at times our friends need us to respond wisely by speaking the truth from God's Word. It's not enough to say, "Everything's going to be okay." Offering those words is like giving someone Tylenol for a broken bone. There might be some immediate relief, but the underlying problem still needs to be addressed. The bone needs to be set, and until that happens, true healing won't take place.

In times of distress, frustration, and confusion, there's nothing our friends need more than God's Word. The most caring and helpful thing we can do for our friends at such times is to speak the truth in love. Of course, Scripture shouldn't be used like a club to smack our friends back into reality! Our words should overflow with the gentleness and humility of Jesus.

Is your friend struggling with a sin? God's will as revealed in Scripture applies. Is your friend suffering? Scripture is a wonderful comfort. Is your friend confused or thinking in a way that strays from the gospel? Go to the Word. By reading our Bible every day, we are prepared to offer true encouragement to our friends, no matter what they're walking through. Don't rely on your own words to encourage your friends; instead, rely on God's Word!

Quiet Time Affects Our Work

During my junior year of college, I started working at a local clothing store. Night after night I showed up for my shift, folded clothes, cleaned changing rooms, and rang up customers.

I was so excited when I was offered the position. It was my first real job, since all my previous work had been contract

Shawni's Quiet-Time Story

I've learned over the years that your quiet time doesn't have to look perfect! We get consumed with what we see in other people's lives and how they spend time with God. Our time with him may look different, and that's okay. It may not be at the crack of dawn, while the kids are asleep; maybe it's in the middle of the afternoon, when they're awake and vibrant. It's okay for them to see you spending time with God, because they'll mimic what they see. At a very young age, my son began asking for Bible time and bubble baths because that's what he saw me do.

labor—filming videos, designing logos, or helping plan and coordinate weddings on the weekend. I'd never gotten an official pay stub before, and it all felt oh-so-official and fun.

That feeling lasted a week.

It wasn't long before I began to dread going to work. The walls felt smaller, the customers seemed less pleasant, and the smells that wafted through the vents from the sandwich shop next door grew old. My rose-colored glasses were officially off, and I found myself dragging my feet every time I had to step inside those sliding glass doors.

But God had something to teach me in this season. The real battle didn't begin when I showed up for work; it began when I opened my Bible in the morning. During my quiet time, God started transforming my perspective about work. He wanted to take me from misery into God-honoring joy.

In our culture, it's common to see work as either a necessary evil or as the sum of our identity. On one hand, we're told that we should "work for the weekend" and then daydream about retirement. Yet this perspective removes the value and dignity from our work *now*. On the other hand, we feel pressure to base our worth and status on our career accomplishments (or lack thereof). In truth, work was never intended to define us or bring us ultimate satisfaction, regardless of whether that work is done behind a counter, at a desk, on a stage, or at a kitchen sink. There will be moments when we wonder, *Is this all there is?* When those doubts arise, we can find comfort in remembering that every labor, big or small, is meaningful and pleasing to God when it's done for his glory and for the good of others.

Work was created by God himself. Before the Fall, God called work "good" (see Genesis 1:27-31). When we work, whether that's in the context of an official job or the serving of our families and communities, we are revealing a beautiful aspect of God's character to the world around us. If we view work as a curse instead of a blessing, we forget that God himself works and creates, and he has created us to do the same in his image. In order to maintain a biblical mindset about work, we need to view it through the lens of God's Word. This will lead to a renewed sense of joy in our labors.

A regular quiet time can also help us as we relate to our coworkers and employers. It can be tempting to view our coworkers as annoyances to endure and our employers as superiors to impress. But if we regularly spend time with Jesus, he will help us see those we work with as people to love and introduce to Jesus.

Ultimately, our work is done for one master: Jesus (see Colossians 3:22-24). As my husband likes to put it, "Having a daily quiet time is like rereading your company's mission statement. It grounds you again in *why* you're going to work every day and *who* exactly you're doing it for."

Quiet Time Affects Our Marriage

If you're married, you know that a relationship with a spouse is unlike any other relationship on earth. However, marriage was never meant to be our ultimate source of satisfaction.

All too often we expect our spouse to fulfill our every need and desire. Then when dissatisfaction inevitably arrives, we think we've made a horrible mistake and we start blaming our spouse or looking for satisfaction in other places. In reality, our problem is not our spouse but our relationship with God.

A regular time with Jesus helps us to keep marriage in its proper place. If we look to Christ as our ultimate fulfillment and joy, we won't be dismayed by the disappointments and frustrations of marriage. It may sound simple, but if you really want to protect your marriage from the seductions of sin and remain faithful to your spouse in body, mind, and soul, then establish and maintain a daily quiet time with Jesus. The Lord uses our spiritual disciplines to keep our wandering hearts bound to him and subsequently bound to those we are in covenant with. No marriage can fail in which both husband and wife are making Jesus their truest delight and utmost treasure.

A daily quiet time can also guard marriage against other harm.

Five months after getting married, Matt and I experienced World War III right in our living room. It wasn't really a "fight," per se, but an evening filled with hurt feelings, raised voices, and lots of tears. The worst part about this emotional explosion was that it was all my fault.

Shortly after getting married, I had unconsciously started critiquing Matt's flaws more than I praised his merits. He didn't walk with the Lord as closely as I thought he should, and I wanted him to be a certain kind of husband—to read his Bible and pray like I did, and to be the "spiritual leader" in our marriage. As a result, I became the nagging and quarrelsome wife talked about in Proverbs 21:9. Increasingly, our home became filled with the tension of my unmet expectations.

At first, Matt tried to comply and be the husband I wanted him to be. He strained to develop spiritual disciplines overnight and eventually exhausted himself beneath the weight of my regular criticisms. After five months, he just couldn't do it anymore. In a fit of exasperation, he let out all his pent-up hurt and frustration. We argued and cried until long after the sun went down, and by the end of the evening, I finally saw how terribly I'd been treating him. I was horrified to realize that my unrealistic expectations were making Matt feel like a constant failure. Instead of being my husband's helpmate and encourager, I'd become his critic and "coach" (a husband's worst nightmare). That evening was a painful but necessary wake-up call for me.

Though I hadn't done so consciously, I had wrongly assumed responsibility for molding and shaping my husband's character. Thankfully, after my wrong mindset came to light, Matt and I were able to start healing our relationship, and I used my newfound understanding to love my husband better. I came to understand that God cared about Matt more than I did and that my quickness to criticize him and slowness to pray for him revealed my own lack of faith in God's power to change my husband.

My job as a wife was not to be the Holy Spirit for Matt but to love and support him as I remained close to Jesus myself. Although I still had hopes for Matt to grow in his walk with God, I now took those desires to the Lord. I also began to focus my interactions with Matt on what I loved about him instead of what I thought he was missing. I offered constructive criticism only when he directly asked for it. I also tried to leave our differences at the foot of the Cross.

As this became our new normal, we started to enjoy each other more than ever. What's more, the Holy Spirit began to work in both of us in ways that surpassed my wildest hopes.

In the years since that emotional evening in our apartment, I have witnessed how graciously the Lord answers the prayers of a wife. As I have humbled myself, surrendered control, and left my husband's development to the Holy Spirit, God has answered prayer after prayer.

There's no better way to protect and nurture your marriage than by spending time in the Lord's presence.

Quiet Time Affects Our Children

Children are smarter than many adults give them credit for. While their ability to communicate and process emotions may be limited, kids are intuitive and insightful. They can tell when adults are lying to them, treating them unkindly, or living hypocritically. If an adult says one thing but does another, a child instinctively understands what the adult is actually saying.

This also means that children are more likely to learn by

example than by being told what to do. If Mom says, "Eat your vegetables" but doesn't eat the vegetables on her own plate, her child will note the double standard and resist vegetables too. Children who observe their parents attending church in their Sunday best and then never talking about Jesus at home will see right through the facade. Worse, they may mimic the insincerity their parents model for them. The same is true for healthy habits. Children who watch their mother pray will likely see prayer as a worthwhile part of the day.

Our children learn what's important to us based on the little decisions we make behind the scenes. We may try to put on a show when we're in the public eye, but we can't hide our true treasures from our children. If we devote most of our time, money, and space to looking good, decorating on trend,

Lydia's Quiet-Time Story

I am a young adult doing missions work with a college ministry at a local church. In this ministry role, I have been learning that I need to fill myself with the Lord and ground myself in his Word before I can go out and walk with my students. If I'm mentally exhausted and not investing in time with him on my own, I won't have enough to pour out to other people. I want my time with the Lord to be not just an event to check off my to-do list but an intentional way of life.

collecting our favorite possessions, or watching all the latest Netflix shows, our children will assume that these are the most important things in life. On the other hand, if we make it a point to spend time with the Lord every day, commit to a local church, show hospitality, talk about Jesus, and love others, then we're showing our kids that Jesus really is our treasure.

If you are a mom (particularly a mom with young children), spending time with Jesus is easier said than done. It may be nearly impossible for you to find the "quiet" part of daily quiet time! Kids are distracting and demanding, and often destroy any hope of a silent moment.

However, the answer is not to forsake our Bibles and quit praying but rather to make quiet time something our children can be part of. At the least, our children will watch us spend time with Jesus and come to understand that Jesus is what Mom truly values. At the most, they will come to a genuine faith in Christ themselves and desire a quiet time of their own.

If we are faithful to spend time with Jesus, our children will learn that the Bible is worth reading and prayers are worth praying, and that neglecting these habits would be like forgetting to brush our teeth or get dressed for the day. Our goal as Christian parents should be to make Jesus such a natural part of our lives that our children come to see him as another member of the family.

As a brand-new mother, I still have much to learn about passing on a legacy of faith and quiet time to my children.

But I have seen what a powerful influence parents can have on the faith of a child. I know, because that child was me.

Throughout my childhood, my parents' faithfulness to read the Word and pray provided an anchor for my own faith. No matter how our circumstances changed, my parents didn't waver in spending time with the Lord. Their quiet-time routine was as firmly fixed as eating breakfast or buying groceries. As a child, I knew that my parents valued their relationship with God as their top priority, and this gave me deep security. I recognized that I wasn't the center of their world, so I didn't feel pressure to perform perfectly for their sake. They proclaimed their love for God with their words, and they proved their love for God with their habits, values, priorities, and actions.

This is what inspires me now that I'm a mom. I want to be the same kind of parent for my children. My hope is that spending time with the Lord every day will plant seeds of faith in the hearts of the generation that follows me.

The Cost of a Quiet Time

There is no such thing as a private faith. Yes, we can kneel in our prayer closets and have a rich relationship with our Savior. But the impact doesn't stop there. Our interactions with God in private will also produce a ripple effect on those around us. Spending time with Jesus allows us to fill our cup with living water, leave our burdens at the foot of the Cross, and then love others as God commanded us to.

Most often, our quiet time will result in joy, harmony,

and depth in our relationships. However, Jesus also warned that our allegiance to him will also bring trouble at times:

> If the world hates you, know that it has hated me before it hated you. If you were of the world, the world would love you as its own; but because you are not of the world, but I chose you out of the world, therefore the world hates you. Remember the word that I said to you: "A servant is not greater than his master." If they persecuted me, they will also persecute you.
>
> JOHN 15:18-20, ESV

Spending time with Jesus is not a magic formula for making everyone like us and ensuring that life is wonderful and easy. Sometimes our relationships become more difficult because of our commitment to Christ. It's also true that loving someone well doesn't often feel peaceful in the moment. Sometimes we have to call out a fellow Christian in their sin, which may result in tension and anger. Sometimes we're led to witness to a coworker who may feel uncomfortable or offended. Sometimes we're called to speak an unpopular truth that brings about a broken relationship. But even when it's uncomfortable, speaking the truth in love is worth the risk.

Our ultimate goal when having a quiet time is to know and enjoy the Lord. Our close relationship with Jesus will ripple out and produce a harvest of righteousness beyond our wildest dreams!

your turn

Read

Proverbs 27:17; Matthew 5:13-16

Reflect

1. Who in your life has a daily quiet time? How has their faith influenced yours?

2. In what ways do you think God might use you to change your corner of the world? What role might your quiet time play in that calling?

Grow

1. If you have a job, write down someone you struggle to relate with at work. Now write a prayer for that person.

2. If you are married, write down one thing you will start praying for your spouse.

3. If you have children in your life, write down what kind of legacy you want to leave them.

Pray

Dear Jesus, thank you for using the influence of others to draw me close to you. Please use my individual time with you to change the lives of others. Help me to be a good friend who speaks the truth in love. As I work, help me to put others ahead of myself.

Please give me the grace to treasure you above anyone else, even my spouse or children. Produce a harvest of righteousness and blessing through my life and faith. Amen.

12

wholehearted love

So Much More than a Quiet Time

I CAN THINK OF VERY FEW ARENAS in which it is admirable to be half-hearted.

No one celebrates a half-hearted athlete.

No one trusts a half-hearted brain surgeon.

No one wants a half-hearted husband.

This value for wholeheartedness is something God ingrained in us. He is not a God of half-hearted efforts or partial love. He is a God who offers us his entire self, and he also wants us in our entirety. He doesn't require our church attendance and then forget about us Monday through Saturday. He settles for nothing less than all of us, the totality of our lives, because he totally loves us.

A quiet time is so much more than something to check off a daily to-do list. During quiet time, we are meant to surrender our lives to Jesus so we can be with him, learn from him, and follow him when our "official" time with him is over. Following Christ is not something to pigeonhole in a particular part of our day but a lifestyle of devotion that's meant to consume our entire lives.

The sobering truth is that anyone can go through the motions of reading the Bible and praying without being transformed. It's possible to read the Bible and not esteem it, to pray to God without actually knowing him, and to practice spiritual disciplines without actually pleasing God with the way we live our lives.

Faithfulness to Jesus is an all-or-nothing choice. We give him either our entire selves or nothing at all.

Faithfulness to Jesus is an all-or-nothing choice. We give him either our entire selves or nothing at all. We submit to either all of Scripture or none of it. God doesn't want us tossing him the leftovers of our lives as an afterthought; he wants our wholehearted and complete surrender.

This means that the Christian faith is so much more than just having a quiet time.

Although regular Bible reading and prayer are vital habits for a Christian, as soon as we limit our devotion to these disciplines, we're missing out on all that God desires for us. The Lord wants us to completely surrender ourselves to him. He wants to do a radical, transformative work in the entirety of our lives! He wants to take his Word and write it on our hearts. He wants to change the way we think by renewing our minds. He wants our relationship with him to become so close that we naturally turn to him in prayer. He wants to walk with us in our homes, in our workplaces, in our churches, and in the world. He wants to be a part of every decision we make.

This kind of wholehearted devotion can't be compartmentalized into an hour of journaling, Bible reading, and structured prayer. Instead, we should be asking God to completely invade our lives and make them over. Bible reading and prayer should be the starting point, not the finish line.

> *Bible reading and prayer should be the starting point, not the finish line.*

Jesus must become the centerpiece of our lives, not just peripheral decor.

From Habit to Heart

There's an important difference between love as an affection and love as a commitment. Our culture advocates that love is primarily a feeling, something that just happens to us and is beyond our control. While there's certainly an emotional aspect to love, the Bible depicts love as an active choice. Whether it's the covenant love of marriage, the self-sacrificing love of parenthood, the unselfish love of friendship, or the radical love for enemies, biblical love is primarily a commitment we make.

The same is true of our love for God. We are not naturally prone to love God with our whole hearts. We naturally love the stuff God has made more than we love God, the maker of everything. Instead of loving Jesus, the Savior of the world, we look to other people or possessions for salvation. In order to align our loves properly, we must retrain our hearts. And to do that, we must retrain our habits.

Not only do our actions reveal our loves, but our actions can also shape our loves. This means that our habits and our loves are inextricably intertwined; each one informs the other. Tim Keller makes this point in his book *The Meaning of Marriage*. He writes, "Our culture says that feelings of love are the basis for actions of love. And of course that can be true. But it is truer to say that actions of love can lead consistently to feelings of love."[8] What we love forms our daily habits, and our daily habits affect our feelings of love. So if our daily decisions and routines are out of sync with where we want our love to be pointed, then we need to change our habits.

> *Our habits and our loves are inextricably intertwined; each one informs the other.*

The rhythms that make up our lives will place us on a trajectory either toward God or toward something else and away from God. This doesn't mean we can't do anything other than read our Bible and pray all day, but it does mean that every other habit needs to be submitted to his authority. When we make the commitment to have a daily quiet time as a nonnegotiable habit, all our other habits and routines tend to fall into their proper places. A quiet time gives us a daily heart check, realigns our soul's compass, and protects us from drifting away from what is eternally important.

The Road Goes On

After being away from my childhood home for about five years, I went on a trip to Mongolia. Matt came with me, and I was able to show him where I grew up, the streets I used to walk down, and the significant places of my childhood. One morning before the sun rose, we walked up the hill to where the old Straw Bale House once stood. Sadly, it burned down years earlier, but the tall wooden fence topped with barbed wire still guarded the beloved yard.

As I peered through the wooden planks, I was able to see the trees my mom had

Moriah's Quiet-Time Story

Becoming a mother showed me that a quiet time isn't about having all the cool devotionals and books but about meeting with God. It's about giving him a few precious minutes of my time so I can thank him and talk to him. It's an altar, not a checklist. So I stopped having devotions and decided to have an altar instead. I try to have my quiet time before I go to sleep at night, but I also pray a lot while I'm doing the dishes! I feel closest to God when I realize that I can't do this life alone. I need the Lord's help for all of it—being a missionary, being a wife, being a mom. I've been learning that it's not about me; it's about God, and his mercies are new every morning.

planted when I was a child. I was also able to see the spot where I'd been doused in the golden light of a dazzling sunset and had believed in Jesus for the first time.

Since those childhood days in Mongolia, I've moved across the world and walked through seasons of rebellion, transition, heartache, and joy. I've seen the reality of my weaknesses, known more fully the weight of my sin, and experienced the mercy of my Savior over and over again. Through it all, my family, my Christian brothers and sisters, and the little stack of books on my nightstand have kept me firmly anchored to Christ. Reading the Bible and praying consistently have been the most important habits in my life, no matter where I've lived or what season I've walked through.

Now in my little city in Central Florida, as I learn to navigate my roles as a wife, mother, and leader of a ministry, I continue to pursue quiet time in the context of a day that belongs entirely to God. Though I am still sometimes tossed on the waves of my own inconsistencies, God's grace always steadies me. He carries the burden for me, helping me walk in unison with him and freeing me from guilt over my failures.

Throughout the ups and downs of my quiet time over the years, I have come to understand that there is no "arriving." Life takes us through countless challenges and changes, forcing us to continually reestablish our time with Jesus. These seasons and struggles are normal parts of life, and the Lord promises to help us as we seek to follow him.

A Burden Lifted

This wholehearted devotion to the Lord—one that encompasses all our loves, lives, and habits—may seem like a daunting ambition. If we view quiet time as something we need to achieve on our own strength, we will quickly burn out. God never intended us to carry the burden of spiritual discipline by ourselves. Instead, we need to remember the gift of grace we've been given. Yes, God desires our faithfulness and wholehearted love for him, and we rightfully pursue these (see Mark 12:30; Luke 10:27). However, through faith in Christ, we are already accepted and blameless before God (see Ephesians 1:7-14; Hebrews 4:16)! Now we can pray like the desperate father who said to Jesus, "I believe; help my unbelief!" (Mark 9:24, ESV).

Even when our faith wavers, even when our obedience is lacking and our habits are far from where we want them to be, we are invited to trust the Savior, whose perfect obedience makes us perfectly right with God (see 2 Corinthians 5:21), who always intercedes for us (see Hebrews 7:25), and whose Spirit lives within us (see John 16:13; Galatians 4:6). Though we are weak, he is strong.

Jesus says that his yoke is easy and his burden is light (see Matthew 11:30). This means that when we are yoked to Jesus, we have his presence and strength to do God's will. It also means that when we fail and stumble, he doesn't condemn us but is gentle with us and helps us get back up. The burden of earning God's favor was removed at the Cross two thousand years ago. And he will finish the good, transformational work he began in all who believe in his name.

New Morning, New Mercies

The other day I sat down with my Bible and journal, hoping to have a nice long quiet time. My hope was short lived, however. Within ten minutes, the baby was up from his nap, my phone had buzzed at least twice, and the dog had thrown up on the carpet. I was initially tempted to become frustrated and discouraged. This was not the quiet time I'd been imagining! But instead of declaring my brief time with the Lord a failure, I decided to put my Bible on my nightstand and move on with my other tasks for the day.

The next day came, and I tried again.

This time I rolled out of bed and decided to knock out a few emails while Matt watched the baby. I figured I'd have my quiet time later in the morning or over lunch. Before I knew it, though, my time was up and Cove was in my arms, loudly demanding my complete attention. The hours filled with household chores, diaper changes, and playing with the baby on the living room floor. Even when I did have a quiet moment, I chose to do work, scroll social media, or pop on Netflix. Soon enough it was time for bed, and I hadn't spent any time with the Lord.

Guilt started to speak to me. *You're such a fraud! How can you tell others to have a quiet time when you didn't even have one yourself today? You aren't qualified to talk about reading the*

Bible and praying—just look at how you wasted your free time! Years ago I would have listened to that voice and allowed it to plunge me into discouragement and shame.

But not anymore.

It's true: we all experience moments of failure, forgetfulness, and frailty when it comes to spiritual disciplines. I come face- to-face with my own inadequacy and sinful nature on a regular basis, so it shouldn't come as a surprise when my self-discipline fails. That's when I remember that Jesus came for the sick, the weak, and the broken, not those who are perfectly self-disciplined or put together. This is the power and beauty of the gospel, that "while we were still sinners, Christ died for us" (Romans 5:8, ESV). Mercy isn't something we achieve; rather, it's something we receive.

So when guilt knocks and shame starts creeping into my

Lucy's Quiet-Time Story

One of the lies I've believed about quiet time over the years is that it doesn't count if I don't have a "sit down" time for at least an hour a day with a book study and a journal. While that's beneficial, it's not the only way to connect with God. I feel closest to God in his creation. Being surrounded by the Father's handiwork puts me at rest and makes me yearn for the day when we will walk with him in the garden again. I've found that whether I have my sit-down time with the Lord or not, he speaks to me by surrounding me with peace, bringing songs to mind at just the right time, and meeting me where I am. God is reminding me that I don't need to initiate resting at his feet. I am already there.

soul, I know who to run to. "My life is hid with Christ on high," as the old hymn goes. He is the one who removes my failure and declares me innocent. Now the Father is not someone I avoid when I fail, but my hiding place, my refuge, my Rock of safety and hope. Now I can look guilt in the face and say, "Yes, I've failed, and yes, I'm a sinner. But Christ is a great Savior, and I will wake up tomorrow to his mercies anew!"

That night I whispered a short request before drifting off to sleep: "Lord, help me to spend time with you tomorrow."

The next day, I opened my Bible as soon as Cove went down for his first nap. My soul was desperately thirsty for Jesus! Thankfully, Cove slept for a full two hours that time, and I was able to have a long, uninterrupted time with the Lord. I happily journaled, read through my entire Bible passage for the day, and prayed without distraction. What a gift! I felt refreshed for the rest of the day.

The reality is that spending time with Jesus will look different in various stages of our lives. Some days will be full of interruptions and discouragement, and we will have to fight hard to draw near to Christ. Some days we will forget altogether, and other days it will seem like our Bible reading and prayer time just falls into place. But no matter what kind of day we're having, our need for Jesus never diminishes. He gives us grace on the hard days, mercy on the failed days, and overflowing joy on the days when our quiet time happens just the way we want it to. Eventually, all these days will fall away as we stand before Jesus on the threshold of eternity. In that moment, our faith will be made sight, our weaknesses and failures will be washed away for good, and the presence of Christ will be ours forevermore.

This is what having a quiet time is all about: knowing Jesus, loving Jesus, and enjoying Jesus. Though we have a while to walk in the shadowlands of this world, we can set our gaze on eternity by reading the Bible and praying. These small, seemingly ordinary disciplines are nothing short of divine, and the Lord promises to help us know and love him more as he leads us heavenward.

your turn

Read

1 John 5:1-5

Reflect

1. In what ways do you want your time with God to go from habit to heart?

2. What burden have you been shouldering alone that Jesus never intended you to carry? What would it look like to surrender that to the Lord?

Grow

1. As you've read this book, what has the Holy Spirit been convicting you about? Write down three mindset shifts you'd like to make, as well as three habits you'd like to implement.

Pray

Dear Jesus, thank you for being a wholehearted God. Thank you for never stopping short in the love you give. I'm sorry for keeping parts of my life from you and for not trusting your complete goodness and love. I surrender all of myself to you and ask that you would do a transforming work in every aspect of my life. May I never stop reading the Bible and praying, and may this habit overflow into the rest of my life. Thank you for your amazing grace, and be with me as I walk the journey of following you. Amen.

recommended resources

THE FOLLOWING ARE RESOURCES that have been helpful to me in my journey of developing spiritual disciplines. This is by no means a comprehensive list but simply a few of my favorite tools that have encouraged me in my walk with Jesus.

Bible Reading

- The Navigators (website): navigators.org
- Bible Gateway (website): biblegateway.com
- Bible App (app): bible.com
- Dwell Bible App (app): dwellapp.io
- YouVersion (app): youversion.com

Bible Study

- Blue Letter Bible (website): blueletterbible.org
- *Women of the Word* by Jen Wilkin (book)
- *Rose Book of Bible Charts, Maps and Time Lines* (book)
- Precept Austin (website): preceptaustin.org
- Logos (software): logos.com

Prayer

- *Prayer* by Timothy Keller (book)
- *You Can Pray* by Tim Chester (book)
- *A Praying Life* by Paul Miller (book)
- *One Thing I Ask* by Hosanna Revival (journal): hosannarevival.com
- Val Marie Paper prayer journal (journal): valmariepaper.com

Scripture Memorization

- Verses (app): getverses.com
- The Bible Memory App (app): biblememory.com
- Remember Me (app): remem.me
- *An Approach to Extended Memorization of Scripture* by Andrew Davis (book)
- *Topical Memory System* by the Navigators (book)

Journaling

- *Quiet Time Companion* by Wholehearted: wholeheartedquiettime.com
- *Give Me Jesus* journal: wellwateredwomen.com
- *The Community Bible Reading Journal*: thecbrjournal.com
- *Abide Journal* by Daily Grace: thedailygraceco.com

Podcasts

- *BibleProject Podcast*
- *Journeywomen* with Hunter Beless
- *Verity* with Phylicia Masonheimer
- *Solid Joys* with John Piper
- *Daily Grace*
- *Risen Motherhood*
- *The Alisa Childers Podcast*
- *Knowing Faith*
- *The Deep Well* with Erin Davis
- *Prayers of Rest* with Asheritah Ciuciu
- *Daily Thunder* by Ellerslie
- *Set Apart Girl* with Leslie Ludy
- *Deeper Christian* with Nathan Johnson

Videos

- The Bible Project: bibleproject.com
- Coffee and Bible Time: coffeeandbibletime.com
- Revive Our Hearts: reviveourhearts.com
- Girl Defined: girldefined.com
- Ellerslie Discipleship Training: youtube.com/setapartlife
- Deeper Christian: youtube.com/deeperchristian

acknowledgments

ALL MY THANKS AND PRAISE to Jesus Christ, who called me out of darkness and into his marvelous light! Walking with you, Lord, is the greatest joy I've ever known. You have held my hand and guided me so gently throughout the years, and it is only by your power and grace that the words of this book were written. Thank you for loving me so patiently and faithfully. To you alone be the glory!

To my husband, Matt: You will forever be the unsung hero behind this book. Without your commitment to provide for our family, this book would not exist! I could list a hundred ways you have served me, supported me, and pointed me to Christ. You are my best friend, my teammate, the love of my life, and my favorite person in the world. Thank you for being such a loving husband and father.

To my parents: Mom, your encouragement and hands-on help while I wrote this book cannot be measured! Thank you for the hours you spent watching Cove so I could write. Thank you for the evenings and afternoons you took to pore over my writing and add your own edits. Thank you for praying for me, listening to me, and loving me no matter what. Your influence in my life has kept me anchored to the Cross. Dad, you are my rock. Your commitment to the Lord and your passion for Scripture constantly inspire me! Thank you for years of theological discussions around the dinner table. Thank you for gathering God's people together, wherever you are, to worship and love him. Thank you for leading me and the rest of your children to Christ.

To my son, my delight, Cove: How I adore you! You have helped me see God's love in a whole new way, and I pray that one day you would come to know that love yourself. I pray that you will grow into a man who follows King Jesus and that you will love reading your Bible and praying every day.

To my siblings, Emily, Leigh, Molly, Andrew, Zack, and Cami: There are no other people I would rather do life with! Your friendship fills my world with immeasurable joy.

To the Tyndale team: Your passion for Jesus and the written word is truly remarkable. Thank you for giving me this opportunity to write a book and for being so patient and generous throughout the entire process. I couldn't imagine a better team to work with! Kara, you have become such a sweet new friend in my life, and I have enjoyed every moment working with you. Stephanie, your editing talent turned this book into something truly beautiful, and I have been so blessed by your encouragement and help. And to everyone else who helped design, promote, and prepare this book for publication, I could not be more grateful for you! Thank you for your hard work and servantlike hearts.

To the Wholehearted team: Kennedy, I thank God often for bringing you alongside me to cultivate and grow this ministry. Maddie, your hard work and creativity have blessed me more than words can say. Emily, I couldn't imagine doing this without you! To our team of writers, thank you for using your time and talents to point others to Christ. And Katie, thank you for being my partner in crime when Wholehearted first started. You have blessed me more than you will ever know.

To Greg and Nicole: Thank you for providing a home for me when I first moved to America. Without your hospitality, who knows where I would be! You have become two of my dearest friends.

To Nonnie and Papi: Thank you for being the most wonderful parents to Matt, in-laws to me, and grandparents to Cove! You are our safe place to rest, a home away from home, and a constant help in time of need. I love you both with all my heart.

To Grandpa Allen and Grandma Brenda: Although so much time and distance separate us, you will always be the only grandparents I have ever known and two of my favorite people in the world. Thank you for loving your grandchildren so well and for all the times you came to visit us in Mongolia. I love and miss you both so much!

Lastly, to my prayer warrior team: You are my closest friends and dearest sisters in Christ. Thank you for praying me through this process. Who knows how heaven and earth were moved by your pleas? Though we live all over the country, I am so thankful that our hearts are knit together by the love of Christ.

notes

1. Emily Miller, "Oaks," *Wholehearted* (blog), June 4, 2019, https://
   wholeheartedquiettime.com/2019/06/04/oaks/.
2. I first learned this concept as a child from the late Dr. Benjamin Sawatsky,
   or "Uncle Ben," as we called him. He was the executive director of my
   parents' mission organization.
3. Charles Duhigg, *The Power of Habit* (New York: Random House, 2014),
   17–18.
4. I first discovered this method from Hunter Beless, host of the *Journeywomen*
   podcast (journeywomenpodcast.com).
5. Heather Clark, "2020 'State of the Bible' Report Finds Few Americans
   Read Bible Daily," *Christian News*, July 24, 2020, https://christiannews
   .net/2020/07/24/2020-state-of-the-bible-report-finds-few-americans
   -read-bible-daily/.
6. "Fanny Crosby: Prolific and Blind Hymn Writer," *Christianity Today*, https://
   www.christianitytoday.com/history/people/poets/fanny-crosby.html.
7. Richard Shelley Taylor, *The Disciplined Life* (Minneapolis: Bethany House,
   1962), 45.
8. Timothy Keller, *The Meaning of Marriage* (New York: Riverhead, 2011),
   109–10.

about the author

NAOMI VACARO is the founder of Wholehearted, an online ministry that provides resources and encouragement for Christians who are trying to develop the habit of daily Bible reading and prayer. Wholehearted was created in 2018, along with the ministry's signature product, the *Quiet Time Companion*. Now Wholehearted sells multiple products in their online store, publishes several blog posts a week, and has a team of eighteen women from all over North America who work to provide content for thousands of readers.

Naomi spent her childhood as a missionary kid in Outer Mongolia before moving to Florida to pursue a degree in graphic design. After graduating, Naomi started working as a photographer and traveled the country to document weddings before officially launching Wholehearted. She married her husband, Matthew, in 2017, and in 2020 they welcomed their firstborn son, Cove.

Naomi now lives in Central Florida with her husband and son. She spends her days writing, homemaking, running

Wholehearted, and fellowshipping with family and friends. Naomi enjoys showing hospitality, scrapbooking, gardening, and discussing theology around the dinner table.

Contact Wholehearted by visiting wholeheartedquiet time.com, and follow along on Instagram @wholehearted quiettime and @naomivacaro.

WHOLEHEARTED

create, keep, and enjoy a daily quiet time

✦ FEATURING:
THE QUIET TIME COMPANION

A PLANNER AND JOURNAL FOR DAILY BIBLE
READING AND PRAYER THAT INCLUDES

- SPIRITUAL GOALS
- PRAYER LISTS
- PRAYER REQUESTS AND PRAISES
- SERMON NOTES
- BIBLE READING PLANS
- DAILY QUIET TIME PAGES

visit

WHOLEHEARTEDQUIETTIME.COM

CP1759